A TALE OF TWO RIVERS

Ronald F. Lasko

Schiffer Publishing Ltd
4880 Lower Valley Road • Atglen, PA 19310

Published by Schiffer Publishing, Ltd.
4880 Lower Valley Road
Atglen, PA 19310
Phone: (610) 593-1777; Fax: (610) 593-2002
E-mail: Info@schifferbooks.com

For our complete selection of fine books on this and related subjects,
please visit our website at **www.schifferbooks.com**.
You may also write for a free catalog.

This book may be purchased from the publisher. Please try your bookstore first.

We are always looking for people to write books on new and related subjects.
If you have an idea for a book, please contact us at ***proposals@schifferbooks.com***

Schiffer Publishing's titles are available at special discounts for bulk purchases for sales promotions or premiums. Special editions, including personalized covers, corporate imprints, and excerpts can be created in large quantities for special needs. For more information, contact the publisher.

In Europe, Schiffer books are distributed by
Bushwood Books
6 Marksbury Ave.
Kew Gardens
Surrey TW9 4JF England
Phone: 44 (0) 20 8392 8585; Fax: 44 (0) 20 8392 9876
E-mail: info@bushwoodbooks.co.uk
Website: www.bushwoodbooks.co.uk

Library of Congress Control Number: 2013936751

Designed by Mark David Bowyer
Type set in AlgerianBasD / Zurich BT

ISBN: 978-0-7643-4440-4
Printed in the United States of America

CONTENTS

DEDICATION

John J. Lasko 2nd
(1911-1965)

When I was a boy, despite being the younger of two siblings, Saturday afternoons were spent alone with my dad. In season, we went fishing for trout and, when I was seven, Dad bought me a bamboo fly rod even though it must have been a financial stretch. We fly-fished for trout during those Saturdays and in winter we would spend our Saturdays visiting fly shops in the Hudson Valley and the nearby Catskills of New York. Our favorite was Folkert's Fly Shop in Phoenicia, New York, on our favorite river, the Esopus. We would take winter excursions to the local trout streams as well as the Catskill rivers, calculating what the stream conditions would be on opening day come April, based on ice and snow accumulations. Needless to say, nearly all my allowance and snow shoveling money went to buying flies from the shops in winter. Like most teens, I drifted away from fly-fishing, but always managed a few trips a year with my dad to the Esopus.

Dad died when I was 18.

I think that somehow he knew he did not have long for this world and sensing my interest in fly-fishing for trout he gave me every opportunity to be certain that it would always remain a part of my life and be a place that I could always go to no matter what obstacles life placed in my way.

He succeeded.

Dad, this book is for you.

The author, at the age of 9, and his dad in 1954, with Northern Pike in the Adirondacks. They wish they were holding trout instead.

INSPIRATION

In June 1988, I was touring the American Museum of Fly Fishing in Manchester, Vermont, following a morning of fishing the Battenkill River. I overheard a discussion between the curator and the famous American fly-fishing author Ernest Schwiebert. I had never met Mr. Schwiebert but I had several fly-fishing tapes narrated by him and I recognized his distinctive voice.

During a break in their talk, I hesitated, but then introduced myself thanking him for his many fine works and lamenting that I had none with me to solicit his autographs. He smiled at my accolades as I blabbered on about his works: *Trout, Nymphs, Remembrance of Rivers Past, Matching the Hatch*, etc. And then, like a star-struck schoolboy, I didn't know what to say further. Ernest broke the impasse with a laugh and relaxed me with a request. "Wait here! I have something I want to show you." He proceeded out the door to his car in the parking lot while the curator and I shrugged to each other in wonder. He returned in minutes with an original manuscript titled "A River for Christmas." He escorted me to the museum library and sat me down. "Please take a good look at this and give me your thoughts. Take your time. I'll be back in an hour or so."

In disbelief here I was, an unknown person whom Schwiebert had never met, touching the pages and reading an unpublished manuscript by the legendary master! As I leafed through the essays perspiration was seeping through my shirt and down my back and chest. My hands trembled and my knees shook. I kept my handkerchief at the ready to stop perspiration from dropping from my forehead and staining the pages.

I don't know how long I reviewed the manuscript, but I remember going cover to cover and back again on adrenaline before Ernie appeared at the door asking, "Well, Ron, what do you think?" I began nervously blabbering again and my exact words have been lost in time, but I do remember complimenting the essay on his interview with Roderick Haig-Brown before his death and telling him how important that missing background would be to fly-fishers the world over. And that essay alone made the book, in my humble opinion of course. Finally, he smiled, "Ron, I am meeting with the publisher in the morning. I will pass on your comments and especially the one on Haig-Brown. Wish me luck at getting this published. I would like it out for Christmas." Then he left the museum with the manuscript in hand waving goodbye.

A River for Christmas was on bookstore shelves that Thanksgiving. I never did meet Ernest Schwiebert again and the angling world lost this great writer, ironically, just before Christmas in 2005.

This chance meeting and my nervous reaction instilled in me the desire to begin writing. But I knew I had to write something of value.

That fateful, brief and only meeting with the master formed the inspiration to write this tale about two little rivers that potentially have a large role to play in the future of our New England sea run brook trout.

ACKNOWLEDGMENTS

Without the vision, support and courage of Pete Schiffer, publisher of Schiffer Publishing, Ltd., *A Tale of Two Rivers* might still be a promising manuscript instead of a book. I am honored that it is their first book on fly-fishing for trout.

Thanks to Steve Silverio and Regal Engineering for providing the Regal Medallion Series vise used to photograph the flies.

North Cairn is a Naturalist and the Lead Environmental Writer for Maine's *Portland Press Herald*. She is a longtime nature writer for the *Cape Cod Times*, the former editor of *Cape Cod View,* and a college professor. North reviewed my book proposal and encouraged me to submit it to Schiffer Publishing. I had no idea that North Cairn, at that time, was undergoing a major life transition. While in the midst of her own challenges, she gave up her precious time to help me, because she believed in my book. North Cairn, your unselfish actions will never be forgotten.

Twenty years ago attorney Bob Bianchi introduced himself following my presentation at a Trout Unlimited Chapter. He introduced me to the historic Tihonet Club, where I was humbled by the club pond's difficult trout. While on a trip to Canada, Bob insisted I fish the home pool at his Salmon Camp on the Cains River. Bob has been a lifelong student of statesman Daniel Webster and owns one of the rare 18-volume limited editions of the complete letters, notes, and speeches made by him. Bob shared his volumes and directed me to the fly-fishing passages by Webster relating his 1840s experiences on the Mashpee River. I shared my full manuscript with Bob Bianchi, which resulted in Bob writing the Foreword to this book.

And I owe everything and more to Donna, my best friend of 50 years, and my wife for the last 46 years, who always believed in me, when others doubted, without whose help, encouragement and support there would be no *Tale of Two Rivers.*

My sincerest thanks to Pete, North, Bob, and Donna, who made this book possible.

Ron Lasko,
Trout Cottage
Barnstable, Cape Cod, Massachusetts

FOREWORD

Robert A. Bianchi

Throughout my half century as a fly-fisher, I have enjoyed wondrous opportunities to meet many knowledgeable and famous fly-fishers and fly tiers from both sides of the Atlantic, including England, Ireland, France, the Canadian Maritimes, and across America. Such meetings usually involve a "tipple" or two and the talk invariably gravitates to the inevitable questions: "What is your favorite trout river?" and "What is your favorite trout?"

Each has his or her own favorites. In Great Britain, one may choose the wild brown trout of the placid chalk stream Test or Scotland's broad, swift, rock strewn, mountain river Spey. In Ireland, a fly-fisher may choose the brown trout found in the limestone, spring- fed river Maigue or the sea run brown trout migrating up the short, rocky outlet to enter Lough Currane. American anglers of the Rocky Mountains prefer the rainbow and cutthroat trout of Spring Creek in Idaho or from the upper tumbling Yellowstone River.

When you discuss this topic with fly-fishers on the North American east coast, from the Canadian Maritimes, across New England, New York, Pennsylvania, and through the Appalachian Mountains to the Carolinas, whether they fish calm spring creeks like the Quashnet or swift valley rivers like the Mashpee, (both Cape Cod rivers that are the central theme of this book) their overwhelming choice of favorite trout is the brook trout. And in the too few remaining Northeast coastal rivers, the sea run brook trout.

I have enjoyed the good fortune to fly-fish and catch many species including tarpon, bonefish, and the magnificent Atlantic Salmon. But in my opinion, the brook trout is the best. This fish, particularly in the spawning mode, is as beautiful as any fish that swims. They can only exist in pristine conditions. I argue that, pound for pound, they put up a fight like no other. The adage so very much applies to the brookie: "It is not the size of the fighter in the fight that matters, rather, it is the size of the fight in the fighter." I hooked my first brookie at age eight, in a little brook in the Town of Sandwich, on Cape Cod, Massachusetts, not ten miles, as the crow flies, from the headwaters of the Mashpee and Quashnet rivers, on an old, beaten up bamboo fly rod and a drifted, red ibis fly. Fifty-five years later, I can still recount every detail of the event. I have been hooked ever since.

I have read over a thousand books on fly-fishing for trout and salmon. Hundreds are on my bookshelves. Some are written in a highly technical "how-to" manner, while others focus on the romance of the sport and still others are focused on the ecological, historical, or environmental issues. I can think of very few writers that have been able to blend all these aspects into one book.

I have just had the immense pleasure of reading Ron Lasko's entire manuscript and reviewing his original watercolor illustrations and over four dozen color photographs that depict the beauty of these two rivers and their brook trout both in words and in pictures. Ron has achieved what few other writers have, by skillfully blending romance, history, ecology, environmentalism, conservation, and fly-fishing into one book.

A Tale of Two Rivers is a trout fishing reference book par excellence.

At first blush, one might assume that this book is solely about the Mashpee and Quashnet rivers. It is not. While the rivers are the centerpiece of this marvelous book, the brook trout is the crown jewel.

Ron brings his many years of experience to the equipment to be used, and the type, size, and dressing of the flies. He has added new patterns, never before published, and incorporated the methods and techniques to be used over the four seasons under a wide variety of weather conditions. All of this is done in exceptional detail, with organization and clarity. The "technical types" within our fly-fishing brethren will certainly appreciate his treatment of this aspect of our sport.

This is also a book of history. It tells of the history of the rivers from prior to the arrival of the Europeans to the present date. Of particular interest is his description of the "Daniel Webster" and "Mashpee Club" eras. He describes, in great detail, the near destruction of the sea run brook trout Cape Cod fishery, due to myopic lumber, agriculture, and cranberry bog practices, and the blocking trout migration caused by dam sites and mills.

His treatment of the ecology of the rivers and the conservation efforts that have taken place over the years is done in depth and will be an enjoyable read, even to those of little or limited fly-fishing knowledge.

Ron Lasko is truly a renaissance man and a romantic in the purist sense. If you ever have the pleasure of meeting him, and I hope you do, I am sure that you will imagine that you have fallen back in time to a kinder, gentler period. He is a tea and scotch connoisseur, fly tier, gourmet game cook, public speaker. Calm of spirit and unhurried, he is appreciative of the world around him and a lover of nature.

Since I began fly-fishing in 1957, I have seen the sport take a turn for the worse. As the famous and much loved golfer Payne Stewart once said, "Fly-fishing should be practiced as the 'quiet sport,' in solitude, in pristine places, relaxed and relaxing." Sadly, to a great extent, our sport has drifted away from that place. In my opinion, this book assists in reemphasizing the attraction of the sport as one of simplicity, enjoyment, relaxation and "quiet."

I highly recommend this book to men and women, on both sides of the Atlantic and the Pacific, from expert anglers to those who have yet to pick up a fly rod or hook a trout, and to all lovers and defenders of nature and the environment.

A Tale of Two Rivers by Ron Lasko is a "GEM."

I am honored to have been chosen to write this foreword.

Tight Lines,

Robert A. "Bob" Bianchi, Esquire
Barnstable, Cape Cod, Massachusetts
August 8, 2012

Bob Bianchi is Past Director of the Atlantic Salmon Federation, Current Director of the Miramichi Salmon Association, Executive Committee Member of The Tihonet Club, member of the Flycasters of Boston, and owner of The Brophy Place, Cains River, New Brunswick, Canada

PREFACE

Maybe a preface should begin with the question: why this book? Why another book on fly-fishing and why a book about two little rivers on the island peninsula of Cape Cod? What is significant or important for this book? These questions have challenged me over the last dozen years as I contemplated writing this book.

Above all else this book is both important and significant because of the unique species of sea run brook that inhabit these rivers. These are brook trout that continue to survive and endure against all the past and present obstacles that man heaps upon them, seemingly bent on their destruction. Sea run brook trout, following the last ice age, and earlier, once existed in hundreds of coastal rivers from New Jersey to Maine and limited populations are now found only in a handful of rivers. Two of these, the subjects of this work, are on Cape Cod, the Mashpee and the Quashnet. This book is important because these two little river valleys have been spared, at least for now, from the developer's bulldozer. Sea run brook trout from these rivers are the hope for future transplants to the dozens of other Cape Cod streams and estuaries in their former range, where they have been devastated and become extinct. These two little rivers are the hope for restoring sea run brook trout to all other Massachusetts coastal rivers along with the rest of New England.

But there is more to this tale. This story is important because of the other inhabitants of these rivers: eels from the Sargasso, herring from across the Atlantic, estuary and freshwater baitfish, along with the aquatic and terrestrial insect life, that, combined, are tantamount to the survival of these sea run brook trout. Maybe this book is necessary because too many fly-fishing anglers have ignored the value of fishing these rivers. Many have questioned why I fish for such little trout, how I fish for them and what patterns and tactics I use. Others allege that there are no mayflies to be found, especially on the Quashnet, when over the last 25 years I have found nearly a dozen mayfly species there and nearly all the usual mayfly species on the Mashpee.

This book is important for the diminishing populations of ruffed grouse, woodcock, quail, and turkey, who hold onto these little valleys and fill our days and evenings with the sounds of drumming grouse, whistling woodcock, and the call of bob-white. It is for the trees, the pine, hemlock, tamarack, birch, cherry, maple, and apple, whose buds, blossoms, scents, leaves and fruits greet us each season of the year.

This book is significant for the history and the people who came before us. Picture a native Wampanoag netting herring to smoke and preserve food for his tribe; a pilgrim planning dams and mills to grind corn and wheat, not realizing the centuries of damage his actions would cause to the fishery; or a farmer clearing a cedar wetland to develop a cranberry bog ignorant that he was causing the loss of cool headwater springs that the trout depended on along with other wildlife. Imagine statesman Daniel Webster, who frequently fished these rivers, writing one of his famous speeches streamside, possibly under that same pine tree where you just rested. Can you see the famous Broadway actor, Joe Jefferson, fly-fishing with his fishing friend President Grover Cleveland, both of whom maintained homes nearby and fished these rivers often, or, since the 1960s, a Trout Unlimited volunteer spending his too little free time on a Sunday to help repair man's damage? Now picture a fly-fisher alone at dusk on the river with only the soft sounds of a summer breeze, the swish of his line, and dimpling trout.

As I wrote this book I realized that it is for all of them; the trout, the animals, the birds, the trees, the insects, the valleys, the conservationists, the dreamers and visionaries, and the fly-fishers past, present, and yet to come.

This book is also meant for the despoilers; the unthinking growers, dam builders, chemical polluters, and real estate developers; if only to help expose the folly of their past actions and, hopefully, to help show the way for future positive actions. This book is for all of us and for the hope that these rivers and trout will be there for the future.

Among many other works, John Waller Hills, a member of the British Parliament and a famous English fly-fisher and author of the early 20th century, wrote the 1924 classic, *A Summer on the Test*. In this book, Hills tells us that any fly-fisher of trout who has spent a generation in their pursuit should endeavor to record one's experiences and work to join the list of literary fly-fishing writers in order to pass on the knowledge to future fly-fishing generations.

The pages that follow have been written on the banks of the Mashpee and Quashnet rivers during every month and season of the year, through all kinds of weather, in a variety of journals, as I wanted the flavor and the experience brought as close to you, the reader, as possible.

You will be the judge, determining if this book meets Hills's fly-fisher criteria of knowledge saved and obligation met.

INTRODUCTION

So, who is Ron Lasko? Whenever I see a new book on fly-fishing, I usually ask this question of its author. You certainly have the right to do so here. Maybe I can best answer that question by telling you what I am not rather than what I may be.

I am not a hydrologist, yet I can explain how the lakes, aquifers, springs, and runoff waters work to enable these little rivers to support trout and other species. I am not a botanist, but I know the names of many of the plants, trees, shrubs, and flowers that grow in these little valleys. I can lead you to wild mint, chives, watercress, and, in season, wild grapes, crab-apples, blueberries, currants, and strawberries.

I am not an ichthyologist, but I can tell you about the comings and goings of the sea run brook trout, eels, herring, suckers, and baitfish, some of which you will not find in books or current studies. Nor am I an ornithologist, but I can point out a scarlet tanager or a ruby throated hummingbird and take you to their exact habitats so you may see one. For that matter, I know where to listen for the drumming of the ruffed grouse, the mating dances of woodcock and snipe, displaying wild turkeys, and the calling of quail. And how to find the places they rest along with their dusting and feeding sites.

I am not an entomologist, but I can identify nearly any hatch of mayfly, stonefly, or caddis in the east, and prescribe an appropriate nymph, emerger, dun, spinner, or wet fly pattern, in the various stages, to interest the trout.

I do not tie flies professionally or commercially, although I have tied nearly every pattern style from a simple fur nymph to a fully dressed salmon fly. I can name almost any pattern in your fly boxes and tell whether they are tied properly to float, drift, swim, and fish correctly. I can identify flies by name whether they be of American, British, Irish, or Scottish origin.

I do not build bamboo fly rods but I restore them. I can replace reel seats, grips, guides, ferrules, and revarnish. I have repaired shattered tips and made them work again. Show me a bamboo rod without identifying marks or signatures and I can probably name its maker.

I don't consider myself a good fly caster but I have taught others, including women, who make excellent fly-fishers. Show me the location of a feeding trout and no matter how difficult its lie, I will find a way to get my fly to the fish even though, often, I can't explain the process. I am not a professional guide, but I will bring you to where the trout are found and show you how to catch them, and on what flies at any particular time of the year.

I don't have all those letters after my name like many other authors. I am basically a self-taught man, an anachronism in this day. Some refer to me as an iconoclast, while others have given me other names.

During a lengthy review of my outlined curriculum for the fly-fishing course that I proposed to teach with the educational director of a school, she asked more questions than I imagined necessary. I explained the literature, the flies, the working of the rivers and the lakes, the history of Cape Cod as it applies to trout, the trout species, the tactics, rods, reels, the gear and equipment, stream rehabilitation, conservation and the environment, which, among others, were all topics in my proposed course.

After several hours of questioning she pushed back her chair and looked at me and the final draft I proposed quizzically. "And what do you call yourself?" she asked as her eyes keep shifting from the draft and back to me. "I am a fly-fisher for trout!" I stated proudly. She smiled. "When I was a young girl, my grandfather and father used to take me fly-fishing for trout." She laughed. "They were fly-fishers for trout!" She exclaimed. "No. You are much more. You are a 'Renaissance Man,'" she proclaimed. A bit red-faced and embarrassed, I thanked her and added, "If you see that in me and my work then I will accept the compliment." Then she stated. "My only regret Ron is that I won't be able to take your course myself." The school accepted my program.

In business I have risen to a variety of levels of upper management and executive status. So many positions, in fact, that the head hunters made me tone down my resume because they said prospective employers would either fear my level of expertise or think I was just outright lying. Eventually, I walked away from such positions as too many corporations in recent decades seemed to only understand words like reengineering, restructuring, or reorganizing, as they lost words like ethics and integrity. Besides, developing wealth was never my foremost interest. I only wanted to earn enough to meet my basic commitments to expenses and family while finding time for the arts and fly-fishing, with some pocket money to invest in fly tying feathers, fishing equipment, and fly-fishing books.

What's in a person's name anyway? A CEO once proposed to change all officer titles in the firm from, Vice President to Team Leader or Assistant Vice President to Assistant Organization Responder, along with other ridiculous names too numerous to mention here. When I paraphrased Shakespeare, "A rose by any other name... would it smell as sweet?" the CEO didn't get my drift.

I can tell you that I am a romantic. One CEO accused me of being a hopeless romantic! But as my wife affirms, a romantic is never without hope. When I write, I do know that I find my heart and soul are right there on the page. They just come out. I can't stop them. So maybe the only way you will really know the answer to the question "Who is Ron Lasko?" is to read this book. You will find me here on every page.

I trust that when you finish the last page and sit back in your fireside chair that you will contemplate the whole of this little body of work and you will answer that question.

And should your conclusion be nothing more than a simple, "He is a fly-fisher of trout!"

Then, that my friend, will be enough for me.

PART ONE: THE RIVERS

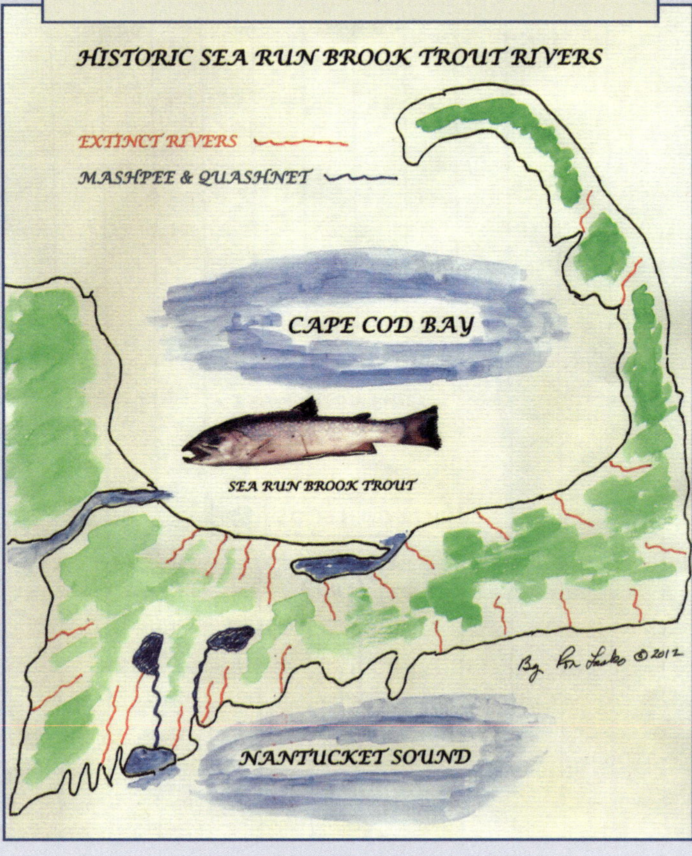

Chapter One

DISCOVERY

This is a story of two trout rivers born out of the last great ice age from melting glacier remains that formed two lakes needing outlets to the sea. Only a mile of land separates the north to south twin flowing rivers. Although they are of the same parents and exhibit similarities, they are as distinctly different as the Beaverkill is to the Letort.

Although their names are followed by the word "River," one needs to qualify that term. Neither is really a river in the general sense of the definition. Each is only three miles in length and averages six to twenty feet in width. I grew up on the Hudson River, which, in sections, is over 4,000 feet wide and is hundreds of miles long. The term *river* is appropriate there. In the Catskills and Adirondacks the term is associated with the Ausable, Saranac, and Delaware, with lesser running waters called creeks, brooks, or streams, or, when in doubt, they are called by one word, such as Willowemoc or Esopus.

An 11″ brook trout resting in a watercress bed on the Mashpee River.

Yet these running waters drain a tiny land mass along the New England coast, the sandy island-peninsula known as Cape Cod. There are numerous trickles hardly worthy of the name brook all about Cape Cod, so in relationship to nearby running waters they were named rivers and therefore I will refer to them accordingly.

I have fly-fished for trout in the big brawling rivers of the Catskills, Adirondacks, across New England, and in the Great Smokies. I have enjoyed the pleasures of the little rivers referred to by Henry Van Dyke in his book; those smaller streams, creeks, brooks, beaver pond outlets, and tributaries of the larger rivers. Often the large, well known rivers have disappointed with their brashness, unwadeable depths, room-sized boulders, and lack of solitude. Too often peace and tranquility are not only diminished but non-existent. In the Catskills and Adirondacks, I often follow the run of a little brook up a mountain or through a valley to find the solitude I seek. I still fish the larger rivers. My favorites are the Battenkill in Vermont, the Esopus in New York, and the Farmington in Connecticut, yet, when I need to get at the reason I fish for trout, I seem to find more answers in the smaller waters.

When we moved to Cape Cod in 1984 from Hartford, Connecticut, I lamented that I would no longer be near my favorite rivers. Distance and time would simply not allow me to fish those rivers as frequently as in the past. I resigned myself to making a few extended fishing trips a year. However, once on Cape Cod, I was pleasantly surprised to hear of two local trout rivers—the Mashpee and the Quashnet. I hastened to see them, but, when I found them, disappointment reigned supreme. "How could they call these little waters 'rivers?' Why, they are not much more than brooks or streams!" So initially I ignored them, focusing instead on my trips to Vermont and New York.

Just as you should not judge a book by its cover, don't ever judge a stream by its size or its view from a bridge. I made that mistake with these two rivers and I continue now to try to make up for lost time.

Chapter Two

FIRST DAYS

It was a vacation that brought us to Cape Cod initially, then another and another until vacation trips to Cape Cod became annual events spanning two decades. True to my nature, our vacations were in the off-season of September and October, when the rush and chaos of the summer tourist season and the crush of people had ended. Oddly, I had given little thought to trout fishing during these visits and never attempted it. Our days were spent tanning and resting on the beaches, with side trips to historical sites and the Islands. Possibly because I had so much wonderful trout fishing in New York and New England, trout didn't mean much when placed in the context of a Cape Cod vacation. I was vaguely aware of references in the guide books to about 30 trout ponds and sea run trout in the estuaries, but passed them off as chamber of commerce tourist come-ons.

A new position in Boston allowed us our lifelong dream of living on the Cape and we moved there in September 1984. It took until November before I could take some time off and explore the Quashnet. The Massachusetts trout season never closes and is open all year round. After following the river from the old mill pond herring ladder for about a mile, I came to an old concrete sluiceway that was still intact except for its wooden dam work, which, in the past, would have been used to flood the once-cultivated cranberry bogs, now overgrown and reforested. I had not yet wet a line and took a lunch break at the sluiceway. I had no idea, at the time, that I would take hundreds of breaks at this spot over the next 25 years.

As I ate my lunch and drank my tea, I noted that the pool here was 4 to 6 feet deep with an undercut, man-made, cedar log crib bank on the west side. The water of the Quashnet had a reddish bronze, peaty color similar to many of the valley streams and brooks I had fished in the Adirondacks. The air was calm, warm, and humid for a November day. My hike had shown many likely holding areas for trout, but I had been more interested in exploring than fishing and had yet to see an insect or a trout.

Lazily, several reddish brown caddisflies began hatching and I watched them intently as they conjured up similar memories of fishing to such hatches on other rivers. Suddenly a fish took one. Then he took another and another, as the caddis hatch intensified. The trout was coming out from the undercut bank to take the fly and then went right back. I tied on a downwing caddis pattern, drifted it down to the trout without casting, twitching it near the bank, and he took. It was a strong, fat, highly colored, 10-inch hook-jawed male brook trout and I released him back to the river. I decided to walk the opposite bank trail back to the old mill pond while looking for hatching insects and rising trout. Halfway back, I finally saw a rise near a barely visible, grassed-over log bank. I repeated the process and promptly hooked and landed a fat, wild, 8-inch brown trout. I saw no other insects hatching or rising trout as I walked the banks back to the herring ladder, but I already knew that these two trout had hooked me on the Quashnet.

I had crossed the Mashpee River many times along Route 130, just below its outlet from Mashpee-Wakeby Lake, while on my way to fish the Quashnet. There are herring ladders here, and the river below looks shallow, but I always wanted to try it. My new position in Boston sent me all over New England and New York and allowed me to fish both my old favorite rivers and a few new ones. After traveling all week, my weekends on Cape Cod turned me into somewhat of a home body, but within one mile of my home in Sandwich I was blessed with a tidal river named Scorton Creek, stocked with sea run brown trout, and a stocked rainbow trout pond named Hoxie. My home fishing spots became these waters interspersed with fifteen minute rides to fish the Quashnet, while I drove past and ignored the Mashpee.

Then one rainy Easter weekend I found myself wanting to fish somewhere other than the Quashnet, but the cold high winds canceled fishing on the open estuary tidal river Scorton Creek or the open waters of Hoxie Pond. I decided to fish the Mashpee River below Route 130 for the first time. There were herring migrating through the fish passage ladders when I stopped at the bridge. The water was fast and shallow looking. I didn't know what to expect, though I reasoned that, since the trout fishing was good in the Quashnet, there ought to be decent trout fishing in the Mashpee. Bundled up in waders and my hooded Barbour coat, with open finger tip mittens and a short fly rod, I entered the river in a secluded wooded section. It was a raw, windy, cold, wet, rainy day. The air temperature was 48 degrees and my stream thermometer read a mere 46 degrees. Not expecting much activity I tied on a size 14 tiny streamer with white-tipped wood duck flank wings. The swift little river was quite a contrast to the slow moving Quashnet. On my third swing through the first deep undercut pocket, I caught a fat, healthy, strong, seven-inch brook trout. These brook trout in both the Quashnet and Mashpee are fat for their size, due to the year-round foods available to them. They are unlike the thin, slender brook trout we are accustomed to find in the mountain ranges of the Appalachians. I continued on down the river fishing every pocket of water, undercut bank, and downed tree.

Five hours later, at the dirt road crossing named Asher's Path, I rested in the rain reflecting on having caught and released over a dozen fat, strong, six- to ten-inch, lovely colored, wild brook trout and having moved or lost at least a dozen others. The conditions were tough and difficult, while fishing flies in such a tightly overgrown stream with tree overhangs was a challenge. And yet, I had enjoyed one of my finest fishing afternoons ever! When I later relayed this experience to a Fishery Division Manager, he speculated that the sea run brook trout I caught were probably returning to the river with the migrating herring after spending time feeding in the saltwater estuary during the winter months.

Back home that evening, as I warmed by the fire with hot tea and a stronger libation, I dozed off with thoughts of all those lovely brook trout.

At last, I had found the sister to the Quashnet River.

The spring creek like lower Quashnet River begins here at Second Sluice where I caught my first Quashnet brook trout in November 1984 as depicted in Chapter Two.

Chapter Three

SEPARATION & REUNION

Now that I had two rivers just a mile apart, I fished every yard of the Quashnet and Mashpee Rivers, alternating between each like the faithful father giving equal time to two daughters. Occasionally I would falter; after discovering a daily hatch of insects on the Mashpee, I would fish her day after day, realizing, after a week, that I had neglected the Quashnet. Then I would make it up to her (the Quashnet) and overindulge until finally feeling a need to get back to the Mashpee and balance things out.

And so went my fishing for several years, with the Quashnet and Mashpee Rivers taking up nearly all my fishing time, and leaving less and less time for my old favorites in New York, Vermont, and Connecticut. In fact, the time spent on the Battenkill, Esopus, or Farmington only made me want to get back to my two little rivers on Cape Cod. Then I accepted an offer to join a new firm as Operations Vice President of the entire southeast of the U.S. I was no longer a 41 year-old failed corporate executive but renewed once again, paving my way to some ultimate prize, whatever that was. It meant abandoning New England, my lovely Cape Cod, and my two little sea run brook trout rivers.

A 10″ fat brook trout caught and quickly released on the Mashpee River using my 1960 6′6″ Orvis Superfine model bamboo rod and English Hardy Featherweight reel.

In Atlanta, I fly-fished for trout in the Chattahoochee all the way from the city to its source in the Great Smokies, where I fished the Pigeon River in Tennessee. Our daughter had remained on Cape Cod, but we flew her into Atlanta year-round for any holiday or excuse for one, and vacationed on the Cape to be with her every June and September. Thus we were able to partially overcome our empty nest syndrome and take in what we missed of New England and Cape Cod a few times a year. During our two-week Cape Cod vacations, I spent most mornings alternating fishing on the Quashnet and Mashpee, and the odd, bad weather, non-beach tourist day would grant me the chance to be their all day. It is not an exaggeration to say that, between vacations, the two little rivers were always on my mind.

Then, in July of my third year in Atlanta, the president of my company came to visit from New York to tell me that he was re-organizing the firm and, although they really appreciated what I had done, they were eliminating my profitable operation to give it to an unprofitable division and that my position and status was eliminated. Within weeks, in spite of other firms offering positions in Dallas, San Francisco, Chicago, and Miami, my wife and I decided to abandon the corporate world and find a way to make a living on Cape Cod. Thus, in August 1991, I returned to my daughter on Cape Cod and began my true education about and attachment to these two little rivers.

We moved within twenty minutes of the two rivers and, having a year round unending trout season, developed numerous opportunities to research, fish, and comprehend their value. I joined the local Trout Unlimited chapter and within months was named to the board as Water Resource Chairman, whose prime responsibility was to organize work parties to clear, clean, and maintain the twenty-five years of stream preservation work that had been performed by past TU members on the Quashnet. Although illness and work pressures forced me to give up my post after two years, I will never regret what I learned about the rivers, their insect life, rehabilitation projects, maintenance, history, and the life of the sea run brook trout.

Fortunately, enough time was allotted to fishing the rivers and, after I healed, I continued to fish and learn about catching the wild sea run brookies, while performing my own small acts of stream maintenance and repair as part of each outing. These activities have resulted in twenty-five years of knowledge about the rivers, the trout, and, of course, how to catch them.

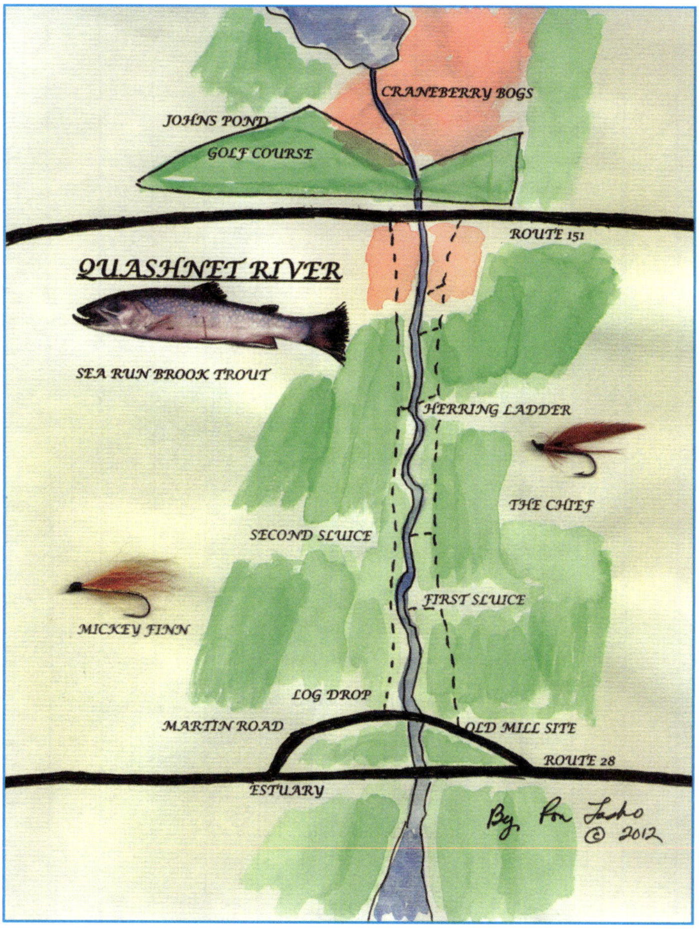

Chapter Four

THE QUASHNET

The origins of the Quashnet River remain the subject of a debate. Some believe it begins in Johns Pond, a trout lake in its own right, either from the herring run-connected brook, constructed and manipulated by man, or from the underground outflow of its glacier-made lake bed, as it is recharged by lens of the Cape Cod main aquifer. Others believe that its origins are actually the multiple springheads bubbling up from the aquifer within the Town of Mashpee-owned cranberry bogs. These bogs were once a large, wild, Atlantic white cedar swamp whose springs, trickles, and brooks converged with any overland outflows or underground seeps from Johns Pond to form a main channel of the Quashnet. The cedar swamp was cut down and bulldozed, then planted with cranberries by the mid-twentieth century, destroying the home of woodcock, wood ducks, grouse, and quail. No matter which theory is advocated, all of the above contribute to form the river. Today, springs still bubble up throughout the 100-acre cranberry bogs, and the trickles and rivulets all converge via man-made trenches and ditches for a half mile, finally forming the beginning of the river at the end of the bogs and the beginning of the Quashnet Valley Golf Course.

Johns Pond Outlet which is the origin of the Quashnet River.

The little river's banks are overgrown as it meanders its way a quarter-mile through the golf course, which was also once cranberry bogs; it is off limits to fishing. The next quarter-mile the river remains overgrown and nearly unfishable. Its hillside banks are flanked by residential development just as it reaches highway route 151. Here the river begins its designation as a catch-and-release stream, using artificial lures only. The regulations should be upgraded to a single barbless fly, but the Fishery division has not been willing to take that step yet. It is strange that the regulations allow one to hook a trout with a spinning lure of multiple treble hooks and attempt to release such a fish, yet a fly-fisher in Massachusetts is only allowed to fish two single-hooked flies at a time. Fly-fishing with a single hooked fly is sensible for preserving the trout populations, especially if they are barbless, and preferable to allowing multiple hooked spinning lures.

Quashnet water treatment plant in cranberry bogs at Johns Pond.

The next mile of the river, after it crosses Route 151, is heavily overgrown and almost unfishable, although it holds trout and has a handful of access spots. The real trout fishing begins after this mile of water crosses an old sluice dam and herring ladder at the gravel fire road crossing. The valley of this entire mile of water had been deforested, bulldozed, and flattened, and the river channel destroyed and then planted for cranberry farming. Vestiges of the old bogs remain along with their trenches, and grouse, deer, wild turkeys, and quail feed in the abandoned bogs on the now wild uncultivated berries. The forest is growing back, but the river bed has been destroyed and this mile is in need of heavy rehabilitation work. Thus the upper river or nearly half of the entire length of the Quashnet, which includes the town-owned bogs, the golf course, and the initial mile south of Route 151, is either off limits or too badly overgrown to fish. But some of its water does serve as a sanctuary and a nursery for its trout because of these conditions.

Quashnet gauging station, Johns Pond

The Quashnet River flowing past a golf green through the Quashnet Valley Golf Course.

The fishable water begins at this herring ladder sluiceway, which was installed and modified to allow passage of herring so they can migrate upriver to Johns Pond and spawn, their eggs hatching to fry and descending the river back to the brackish Waquoit Bay on to Nantucket Sound and the Atlantic Ocean, completing their life cycle. This herring ladder also allows the sea run brook trout to access the upper river all the way to Johns Pond and even may be used in a form of reverse migration by both the trout and suckers who reside or utilize Johns Pond. Anadromous trout and salmon populations, along with resident trout populations, have been studied in recent years in the British Isles where fish migration has been the reverse of what we usually think. These fish rest in the lakes then spawn in the only running water—the outflow. This may be happening with our sea run brook trout as well.

The mile of water below this herring ladder is a typical woodland valley stream generally 6 to 12 feet in width and running calf-deep, but with numerous pockets, riffles, runs, and holes that range from knee to waist deep and even a few that are up to the chest. Scores of clear cold springs enter the river throughout, keeping the temperature at 45 degrees in winter and in the 60 to 65 degree range all summer. Massive tree plantings and log embankments with overhead hides for the trout have been undertaken by hundreds of Trout Unlimited volunteers in this wooded stretch since the 1960s, led by the tireless Fran Smith of Falmouth, Massachusetts. The woods and banks have grown up so naturally that much of this man-made work is no longer visible to the untrained eye. This water has fine gravel runs and small rocks that generally all have been brought in by hand to reconstruct the stream bed. Much of the fall spawning of trout take place in this water and, although it is difficult to dry fly-fish, it is possible for one prepared to fish on one's knees using short 6- to 7-foot fly rods. There are trout holding in most of the likely looking places and, although the average size caught is in the 7- to 8-inch range, one can be pleasantly surprised when one of the small stream 12-inch monsters takes your fly. Bank access is passable by somewhat overgrown paths. But it is the beauty of this wooded section of water and not the size of the trout that is the reason for being here. And it stands as proof that man can help nature rebuild a destroyed river. I love this water.

The restored from cranberry bog to wooded valley upper Quashnet River. Trout Unlimited Volunteers brought spawning gravel and river bed rocks in by hand buckets to recreate this river bed. They planted trees above new log reinforced banks. Today, trout are found along the overhanging foliage and in the undercut banks.

After a mile of gently meandering wooded runs, riffles, and pools through the now recreated, reforested valley, the river slows and the valley opens and widens into what is now a massive marsh and swamp overgrown with bog myrtle, where cranberry bogs once existed following the deforestation and bulldozing of the lower wide valley. The forest retreats to the side hills hundreds of feet away from the river. The gravel bottom now gives way to a sandy, muddy, soft, and mucky bottom. The river widens and deepens. It becomes mainly waist- to chest-deep with only the rare overhanging tree and resembles a small English chalk stream or a small Pennsylvania limestone river, especially during weed season. The trout lie under the muddy brushy overgrown banks in holes and pockets that may be neck-deep; they only cautiously venture out to feed with a wary eye for their main predators—the unrelenting osprey and heron. The river meanders this way for a mile or more all the

The view from First Sluice facing north. This is a favored place for a tea break or lunch. I can watch for rising trout for hundreds of yards all the way to the willows. The rod is an Orvis bamboo model 7/4 fitted with an Orvis reel.

way to Martin Road, passing through several old concrete sluiceways and the broken remains of many more curving from bank to bank, especially where TU has installed log cribbing and hides. The muddy, sandy bottom is unstable and changes with floods. There are some dangerous quicksand-like pockets and it is impossible to fish from the soft boggy banks.

And yet, this water is the best dry fly water on Cape Cod, with this stretch of river allowing one to use longer rods and really let loose one's casting arm and abilities. But it is similar to fishing a spring creek and the trout scare easily. The river passes under Martin Road, where it becomes a solid gravel and rock bottom again for several hundred yards. It then passes under Route 28 and enters the brackish water of Waquoit Bay. At Martin Road, there are the remains of an old mill from the 19th century, whose dam once prevented the sea run brook trout from entering the upper river. This small run of several hundred yards between Martin Road and Route 28 was the only spawning habitat for the sea run brook trout for nearly a hundred years.

At the top center of this photograph is where the Quashnet meets the saltwater estuary known as the Moonakis River.

Here the Quashnet River, now renamed the Moonakis River, enters Waquoit Bay, after which it terminates into Nantucket Sound.

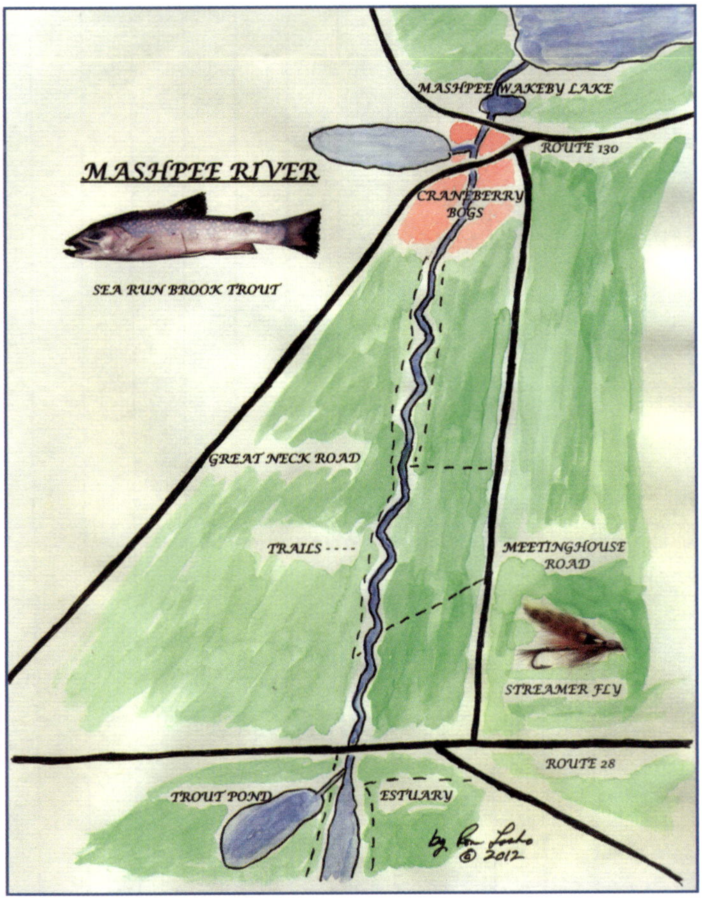

Chapter Five

THE MASHPEE

The Mashpee River begins as an outlet of Mashpee-Wakeby Lake. At the outlet, a low, man-made dam, passable for herring and trout, has raised the level and size of the lake. After its first several hundred yards the river is met by another dam and fish ladder run that creates a small stillwater pond as the river crosses Route 130. After this herring ladder run area, it continues through an abandoned cranberry bog now overgrown with brush as it curves southwest towards the Mashpee Rotary. Just before it crosses the winding Route 130 once again, the river is joined by the outlet of another shallow stillwater pond. Mashpee-Wakeby Lake and these two stillwater ponds contribute their warm surface waters, as high as 80 degrees by summer, to the river, making this section too warm to support trout from June through September.

After Route 130 the river continues its south-southwest meandering along Meetinghouse Road before breaking off in a westerly direction for a quarter-mile through another old, overgrown cranberry bog. Here the river's character is mostly a straight trench, due to creation of the cranberry bogs in the late 1800s. There is little bank holding cover here and no overhead foliage. Despite cold springs entering every 50 feet or so the little river remains too warm to hold trout in the summer. In winter and fall, I have found trout in the entire upper portions of the river, but the holding cover is marginal.

The Mashpee-Wakeby Lake outlet and the origin of the Mashpee River.

Mashpee-Wakeby Lake outlet herring ladder and the origin of the Mashpee River. The chain link fence enclosure is intended to reduce poaching of herring.

The herring ladder, a concrete sluiceway at Route 130 on the Mashpee River.

The Mashpee Wampanoag Indian Historical Museum
located adjacent to the Route 130 herring ladders.

It is high summer on the upper Mashpee River. Shortly after it enters its wooded valley, a swamp maple is turning orange above spotted touch-me-nots, both harbingers of the coming autumn.

Finally, the river enters the heavily wooded and forested valley that maintains a giant umbrella over her for its several mile run to the saltwater estuary of Popponessett Bay. Shade from the hardwood and coniferous trees, along with new springs entering via the surface and the streambed, drops the river temperature to 60 degrees even on the hottest summer days. Trout suddenly appear and can be found in every available piece of cover; undercut banks, tree roots, weed beds, under overhanging foliage, and below sunken rocks and logs. From here, all the way to the estuary past Route 28, the river curves to and fro against its east and west banks as it swiftly runs south towards the sea. The angler fishes under a cathedral-like canopy of 50- to 100-foot high trees in the upper story and then smaller trees along the banks. The banks rise high on each side of the river, a geological feature that saved the river from the bulldozer flattening practiced by the cranberry growers of the 19th century. With each collision of the banks the river carves out deep pockets and undercuts providing homes for our trout. The entire river runs gin clear and its fine rock and gravel bottom throughout its entire length allows spawning nearly everywhere in spite of its swift currents. The river appears similar to the famed Battenkill River near Manchester, Vermont.

Nearly all the famous mayfly hatches, along with the usual wide variety of stonefly and caddis hatches, occur here in season from March to December providing a steady food supply for sea run brook trout fry, smolts, parr, and adults. Besides a handful of home sites where unthinking homeowners have clear cut to the river's edge, the river is the least altered trout stream on Cape Cod. If Daniel Webster's ghost still fished here, he would see this section of the river as it was in the 1830s. Here is truly one of the last places to find limited solitude on Cape Cod.

Because this section of the river, all the way to Route 28, was owned in the 19th century by a private trout fishing club it was never denuded of its trees. Both banks are now part of the Mashpee River Woodlands conservation area and are preserved, although new housing developments have expanded just out of sight, but not out of sound. There are a few vestiges of old log hides and cribbing installed by the private fishing club, as well as the sites where the club created English-like hatchery "stews," where they reared trout and released them in the 1890s, when the fishing diminished due to their own overfishing of the sea run brookies. Today, these several miles remain a quiet sanctuary for contemplative fishing and the angler can imagine himself fishing a wilderness stream anywhere.

After crossing Route 28, the river is joined by the outlet of the small Trout Pond. Here the river is brackish at high tide and freshwater at low tide for an eighth of a mile before becoming mostly saltwater. The cover is diminished as the river begins to widen to become an estuary, but trout can be found here especially whenever they are migrating. Once the water becomes too deep for the wading angler, a canoe will take one all the way to the sea.

The Old Indian Meeting House in Mashpee on Indian House Road across from the lower Mashpee River. It was established in 1684 by the descendents of Massasoit.

Plaque on the Mashpee Old Indian Meeting House. Massasoit was credited for helping to save the Pilgrims in the 1620s. Even though the Mashpee Wampanoag did not fight against the European settlers in the 17th century Indian Wars, they still lost their lands.

Trout Pond before its outlet flows into the lower Mashpee River.

The lower Mashpee River brackish upper estuary at high tide.

Chapter Six

THE TROUT

When the last great ice age retreated, it had piled and left behind huge mounds of sand creating the peninsula of Cape Cod. Heavy deposits of glacier ice were buried in the sand over an underground freshwater aquifer. As the ice melted, the waters created lakes and ponds that were recharged by the aquifer. Many lakes and ponds overflowed and created rivers to the sea while others, called kettle ponds, had neither inlets nor outlets, their condensation loss being recharged by springs and lenses through the aquifer. The char, known today as our sea run brook trout, ranged between the glaciers and their free-flowing, cold, freshwater drainages and the saltwater. When the glaciers dissipated about 10,000 years ago, the sea run brook trout remained behind and populated the freshwater rivers and lakes. They utilized the saltwater estuaries, bays, and the sea to become fat on the abundant marine foods, spawning in the rivers and the headwater lakes to create a new cycle of offspring. As conditions dictated, they learned to feed and grow in both freshwater and saltwater, depending on water temperatures, seasons, predators, and food availability. The char or brook trout that became trapped in the kettle ponds without inlets or outlets adapted and used the gravel spring beds for spawning.

Before man inhabited Cape Cod, the trout's predators were the larger fish at sea, seals and otters in the bay, and fish-eating ducks, osprey, and herons in the estuaries, rivers, and lakes. The native American Indians—the Wampanoags of Cape Cod—fished for these brook trout but never took so many as to deplete their numbers. In fact, all through the thousands of years following the ice age both the Wampanoags and the brook trout flourished in these waters.

In 1620, another predator arrived on the scene—the pilgrims of Plymouth Colony who discovered the brook trout to be of both the size and quantity to be taken as a steady food source. These settlers, however, depleted sea run brook trout not just by eating them, but by building dams and millraces on nearly every free-flowing stream. There was timber to cut and corn, wheat, and barley to grind. Water power was used to run the mills' waterwheels and that required dams. Dams are a death sentence to any anadromous fish population, whether they are shad, herring, eels, salmon, or trout. Our sea run brook trout, for the first time in over 10,000 years, found themselves unable to ascend the rivers from saltwater in order to utilize the rivers for food, protection, and spawning. Thus began their decline, which continues today. Although now most of the dams have either been removed, circumvented by fish ladders, or fallen into decay, due to the 400 years of losing river-specific gene pools, the trout have almost vanished and survive in just a few rivers.

We did not, however, stop at overharvesting the trout and blocking their river access alone. We cut down the forests that provided trees and shade that cooled the rivers, allowing them to heat up intolerably for brook trout. We dug wells into the lenses of the aquifer resulting in diminishing and even drying up the spring flows, which in turn reduced the volume of the little rivers and further warmed them. Our agricultural practices bulldozed the river valleys, altered the course of the rivers, and destroyed the river beds that harbored aquatic insect life and spawning gravel. Then we poisoned the land with fertilizers, pesticides, and herbicides, which drained into the aquifer and into the springs, ending in the rivers, where they added their pollution and poisonous effects to the trout food and the trout themselves. Then we cut a channel known as the Cape Cod Canal and destroyed its two largest sea run brook trout rivers in the process forever creating this island-peninsula. Then we built a giant military base and, through deliberate dumping on open soil, allowed all sorts of chemicals, gas, and oil to drain into the aquifer, then, via springs, into the rivers. Our dump grounds add to the leaching of harmful chemicals, as do the road tars and motor vehicle emissions, and our power plant, making the rivers more acidic from rainwater and further inhibiting the trout's survival ability. But we are not through yet. We have added our own septic waste leaching. We want greener lawns, so we add more nitrogen, fertilizer, and pesticides to achieve the manicured lawn look of suburbia, but ignore that our land is made up of sand and that these things end up in the aquifer and runoff waters. Then we add even more chemicals through our large recreational fields for golf and other sports.

The Cape Cod brook trout had vanished entirely from most rivers, were marginal, at best, in others, and only maintained small populations in a handful by 1900. Man rationalized that we could resurrect the Cape Cod river fisheries using stocked hatchery trout. Over the last 100 years, we have stocked these rivers with hatchery brook trout that lacked the genetic disposition to survive these waters. We stocked exotic hatchery trout such as the west coast rainbow trout and the European brown trout. Most of these stocked trout were oversized for the little rivers. They tend to be overly aggressive and competitive to the native brook trout, further diminishing them.

A strong, healthy, 12" brook trout from the restored woodland upper Quashnet River. This is still a rare trout but they are more frequently found than 25 years ago. The rod is my dad's Catskill-style, restored, 7'6", 1950 South Bend fitted with an Orvis reel.

Most of the bays, estuaries, and rivers of Cape Cod are now devoid of brook trout. They have been eliminated by all these practices. There are only two rivers on the peninsula where sport-fishable populations of brook trout continue to hold on—The Mashpee and the Quashnet. They have withstood the onslaught of mankind, with his dams, his pollution, his ignorance of the natural world, his planting exotic species, and his arrogance towards this incredible species of trout. They have, in recent years, withstood the burgeoning populations of bluefish and striped bass and increasing numbers of herons and ospreys. But housing developments and strip malls at their doorstep have encroached on their habitat, so the future effects still remain to be seen.

Why have the sea run brook trout of the Mashpee and Quashnet rivers survived when man and nature have been so set on destroying them? I asked this question of a former member of the Fish and Wildlife Division who had been a proponent of stocking European sea run brown trout in our Cape Cod brook trout rivers. He acknowledged that in retrospect they had made a mistake. They had undertaken numerous studies in the first half of the twentieth century that indicated that the Cape Cod sea run brook trout were doomed. Their studies concluded that they simply were not tough enough to withstand man's destructive forces and that only the exotic European brown trout could. They wrote off the brook trout's survival, figuring the sea run brown trout would fill the niche. They were wrong. After a 30-year program of stocking sea run hatchery brown trout in numbers and sizes greater than the brook trout populations of the Mashpee and the Quashnet, it is the brown trout who has not survived in the Mashpee and they are now nearly entirely gone from the Quashnet. Fortunately, the stockings of brown trout in the Mashpee and Quashnet rivers ceased in 1993. The resultant growth in both the size of individual brook trout and in their populations has become obvious since 1993.

Our Massachusetts Fisheries Division does an outstanding job of raising our necessary hatchery trout for Cape Cod's trout ponds and they should be commended for their excellent management of these thirty plus trout ponds and lakes, whose brook trout were netted out during the 18th and 19th centuries and eradicated. Today, we enjoy a little known world class lake and pond trout fishery here on Cape Cod thanks to their efforts. They should also be commended for changing their views on the sea run brook trout as they now fully support maintaining the unique strains of the Mashpee and Quashnet

A 10" fresh sea run brook trout from the lower Mashpee River near the brackish saltwater estuary caught and quickly released by the author. These silver-blue brook trout will turn into their regular colors within days of entering freshwater.

through habitat restoration and maintenance. Our Fisheries Management is also studying ways to use these strains to expand the fishery to other historical rivers, in order to resurrect those long destroyed and depleted waters. We can all agree now that Cape Cod's remaining sea run brook trout are tough. After all, they have been subjected to more than their share of obstacles and adversity and they have survived. The absolute keys to successful sea run brook trout fisheries on Cape Cod are protecting existing habitat, creating new habitat, keeping the springs running cool and unpolluted, and practicing catch-and-release, thereby allowing nature and the trout to do the rest.

It is my belief, and that of others, that the thousands of years of genetic development have made these trout micro-habitat-oriented, in that they utilize every aspect of the environment to their advantage. They use the sea, the estuary, the river, and the lakes at different seasons for different purposes. They are not aggressive toward each other and tolerate their brethren. They regularly share prime holding and feeding areas without harassing one another. They are prolific in creating offspring. During the warm summer months, I have even observed them grooming one another of parasites by nipping bloodworms and leeches from each other's fins and gill plates. I have observed these trout tolerating the presence of herring, eels, and other fish life. During the heavy three-month herring runs up and back down these rivers, I have observed a stocked hatchery brown trout drive itself to exhaustion as he harried the migrating herring that temporarily occupied his holding area. Conversely, our sea run brook trout calmly accept these adult herring and even migrate along with them upriver and down, using them as cover and feeding alongside the herring without being threatened.

Another unfortunate occurrence during the heavy brown trout stockings on these rivers was the successful hybrid mating of brown and brook trout, because they spawn at the same time of year using the same river beds. Resultant hybrid offspring are called "tiger trout" and are sterile. Such sterile fish occupied space that should have been taken by reproducing brook trout. Fortunately, with the end of the brown trout stockings in 1993, such instances no longer occur. We must remain vigilant so that such ignorance by fisherman and fisheries personnel is never repeated.

And so, as you fish these rivers and catch these colorful and lovely brook trout, give thought to their 10,000 year history, their survival abilities, and the obstacles they continue to face, and release them gently back to the stream to grow and continue to add to their race.

A 12" wild tiger trout caught and quickly released by the author in the willow bend run above First Sluice on the Quashnet. These hybrid sterile trout occur in the wild when brown and brook trout share the same spawning beds.

PART TWO:

THE SEASONS

Chapter Seven

WINTER

JANUARY

I have come to love my winter trout fishing on Cape Cod. I grew up fishing the Catskill and Adirondacks where trout seasons closed September 30 then reopened April 1. In Massachusetts, January means not only a new year but a new trout fishing year. The whole trout season lies before us and, here on Cape Cod, our little rivers are open all 12 months, so I indulge myself in their pleasures each and every month. January is the time for new beginnings and with a twelve-month season there is no pressure to fish at the fever pace that infects anglers whose season begins in April or May. In January, we fish at a leisurely pace and in solitude. We have the rivers pretty much to ourselves, mainly due to the weather and the average trout fisher's belief that trout fishing isn't good until May. Oh, what they are all missing!

January days can be 50 degrees or -10. They can be sunny and warm or too bitter cold to even step outdoors. So one must always have the trout fishing gear ready to go and be poised to grasp the opportunity whenever nature and weather allow. Even on pleasant days one must be fully and properly dressed because, as Mark Twain once cautioned, "In New England the weather changes every five minutes!" We may start out in a pleasant, warm sunny noon of 50 degrees only to find ourselves in 30 degrees with snow by 3:00 PM. The river temperatures vary slightly, between 42 and 46 degrees. One needs long underwear, wool pants, and fleece overpants under the insulated boot foot waders in order to stand these cold water temperatures for an hour before needing a warm up. Wool fingertip mittens are an absolute necessity. Bring an extra dry pair as, if the gods smile upon you and the trout are coming readily to your flies, your mitts will become wet and cold quickly. Having a spare dry pair has made the difference in extending my fishing through the afternoon or heading home early due to frozen, numb fingers unable to handle a line. Hand warmers will also be needed and useful.

The Quashnet River in winter.

Two out of every three January days will bring clouds and precipitation in the form of a cold wet rain, sleet, or snow. A waxed cotton, Barbour-style coat with matching hood is needed to keep out the moisture and retain body warmth. I wear mine over a cotton turtleneck under a wool Irish fisherman's sweater, which is under a heavy chamois shirt. A wool Irish fisherman's tweed hat will keep your head warm. A neck choker towel will help keep out moisture. Now I am ready for any weather condition. I find great pleasure in my warm gear and the time it allows me to keep fishing in the winter while others are confined to their wood stoves. A waxed cotton shoulder bag carries my lunch and a thermos of hot tea. Taking a break from fishing along the river to watch snowflakes fall, while sipping piping hot tea, is one of the finest of pleasures we winter fly-fishers can treat ourselves to.

But you may wonder...can we really take trout on flies in January? But of course! January is the month of the black midge. They are hatching and are on the water nearly every day, ranging in hook size from a 14 down to a 28. All during the month, shiners, sculpins, and stickleback baitfish are available. In late January, size 16 and 18 tiny winter black stoneflies are hatching, signaling the larger stonefly hatches to come. Slowly fished Black Gnat wet flies and a variety of streamer patterns have proven effective.

I listen to hear the birds singing louder and more often as they try to impress potential future mates. As I round a bend in the river, I hear the sudden flush of a ruffed grouse from the stream bank; it pleases me that he has survived both the hunting season and early winter and will be parenting more grouse. The predatory herons and osprey are gone to warmer climes. The weather is too cold for them and we are thankful that our trout receive a respite from these relentless pursuers. The few trout we catch remain healthy and fat. There are many nymphs active on the river bottom, along with scuds and freshwater shrimps to balance their intake of baitfish. At times severe cold snaps freeze the estuaries and bays and we find wintering-over black ducks deep up our river valleys, using the river's open, warmer, spring-fed waters.

It is wise to keep another hot thermos of tea back at the car, along with a complete change of dry clothes, including undergarments and socks. Hypothermia is a real threat and dangerous when fishing in the winter. Warm tea and dry clothing have saved both a fishing day as well as my health, whenever 45 degree water has gone over my wader tops or I have fallen in. Sooner or later we all get wet, so be prepared and carry some dry towels and a first aid kit in your vehicle as well.

Towards the end of January we make the great discovery! We find freshly hatched trout fry in the shallows. They dart away among tiny weeds, watercress, sand, and bits of leaves, disappearing as quickly as we spot them. If we are fishless, no matter. We know the adult

A 10" fat brook trout caught and quickly released in January on the lower Quashnet River. Even in winter these trout are fat and healthy, so unlike the thin brook trout of mountain streams. The rod is a 6'6", 1960, Orvis Flea with a tiny Orvis CFO-1 reel.

trout are there. We know the trout fry are beginning to hatch, promising that our unique species of sea run brook trout will be renewed. They represent the future trout and our future fishing. We are careful not to disturb them or worry them needlessly. As we take the path back to our car and hot tea among falling snowflakes, we are satisfied that life is as it should be, whether we caught any trout or not. There is no ending to life or to our trout fishing—only renewal.

FEBRUARY

More often than not, February roars in like a lion with temperatures below freezing, hurricane-force winds, snow, and below zero wind chills keeping us from our rivers and fishing. Fortunately our island-peninsula is surrounded by Gulf Stream ocean water that rarely falls below 44 degrees. All it takes is a southerly flow of air and our days warm to near 50 degrees. The days are longer now, as we have gained 90 minutes of daylight since December. This alone raises our river water temperatures to 46 degrees, on average, making both fish and fisherman more active.

Three major events occur in our rivers during February that vastly improve our fishing. The first is the arrival of the newly hatched elvers migrating from the Atlantic Ocean area named the Sargasso Sea. These elvers enter our rivers where they will feed and grow over a period of years before returning as mature eels to the Sargasso to spawn. The continuous hatches of the tiniest black midges provide food to the colorless, cellophane-like elvers, who begin to gain color as they feed. These elvers become a major winter food source for our trout. Imagine their glistening, slender, transparent bodies touched by sunlight and filled with black midges as they swim about in undulating motions attracting the trout. I believe the elvers are responsible for the success of the Black Ghost streamer in New England rivers that are accessible from the sea. Its black body, spaced in silver tinsel, white wing, yellow tail, and throat hackles, with jungle cock eye is the perfect elver imitation from winter into spring. Another effective pattern is the Light Spruce streamer, with its splayed, dark-stripped, silver, furnace hackle wings working in and out on a stop-and-go retrieve. The trout feed heavily on these elvers and with improving water temperatures readily take our tiny Black Ghosts and little Light Spruce streamers.

The second major event is the complete hatching of the trout eggs, as we find thousands of trout fry everywhere. These fry spend their time in the shallows feeding on plankton and tiny midge larva in the detritus of the river bottom. If you wait patiently and silently out of sight, you will see the shallows come alive with feeding trout fry and feeding trout, too! Yes, some of our adult trout are cannibalistic and, in addition to feeding on the elvers, we see them lying in shallow water, sometimes with their dorsal fins out of water as they pursue and feed on the thousands of trout fry. These one- to two-inch trout fry are surprisingy highly colored. Their tails and fins are orange-red, and parr marks are clearly visible. There are red, orange, yellow, green, and blue dots, along with early vermiculations on their backs. Their eyes stand out clearly and their gills flash red. The time-honored Grizzly King streamer with its red tail & throat hackle, pale green-gold tinseled body, and grizzly wings is a most suggestive pattern that is effective on our opportunistic adult trout. Tying this pattern with splayed wings gives it more action and better results when fished in slower water.

The third major event is the hatching of the early black stoneflies by mid-month. They are a good size, requiring a number 12 or 14 hook, and, once they begin hatching, you will find them on the water nearly every day from 10:00 AM until dusk, weather permitting. For the first time since early November, you will actually find trout surface-feeding to these hatches and spinner falls, with you taking your first dry fly-caught trout of the new year. Although the adult insect's wings are pale gray they appear white on sunny days. A traditional wet Black Gnat pattern has proven deadly during these hatches. Tie up a few with yellow egg sacs to represent drowned egg laying adults. For fishing dry I like a Leonard Wright-styled down wing fly pattern, using pale gray mink tail fibers for the wings, a black fur body, and a dark dun hackle collar. When the hatches are heavy at times you will find surface feeding trout so selective that they will only take a floating adult when it raises its wings in an attempt to fly off. The still floating down wing stoneflies are ignored by our full-bellied trout. At such times a traditional up wing-styled dry fly Black Gnat is the secret for catching these picky well fed trout.

In fact, I believe we have abandoned too many of our up wing dry fly patterns in recent decades for modern down wing patterns. I have witnessed this phenomena of trout selectivity during heavy hatches of down wing midge, caddis, stonefly and down-wing ants, along with floating mayfly spinners on these rivers as well as on the Esopus in the Catskills, the Battenkill in Vermont, the Farmington in Connecticut and the Ausable in the Adirondacks. Well fed trout seem to only want the fly trying to get away! The up-lifting of the wings of such normally down wing insects triggers the trout to rise. On such days and on such trout the old up wing dry flies tied with hackle tips or duck quill sections are deadlier than our modern down wing patterns. When I look into most fly catalogs, I am afraid that we have thrown the baby out with the bath water, as it is getting increasingly difficult to find any of the traditional up wing dry fly patterns.

Although snowstorms and sudden arctic cold fronts prevent us from fishing on some days, the equation swings in our favor in February. There are more sunny days and more days hitting high temperatures of 45 to 50 degrees than any time since November. The water temperatures may fluctuate with the weather but, by month's end, some days it hits 49 degrees and our wild brook trout under these warming periods feed all day on elvers, trout fry, and early black stoneflies, giving us opportunities to take many trout in spite of our heavily bundled up bodies.

Ah, beautiful winter!

Chapter Eight

SPRING

MARCH

March 1st is, to me, the very first day of spring. I don't care what the calendar says. By the first of March our little rivers are alive with multiple hatches of a wide variety of midges, stoneflies, and caddis.

The continuous hatches of midges now include a cornucopia of colors: olive, maroon, yellow, and cream are coming mixed in with the predominant blacks and all in a variety of sizes from #14 to #28. The tiny #16 black stones keep coming along with our #12 and #14 early blacks. The early brown stone #12 now also makes its appearance along with the little red stonefly. Joining these are the #16 dark brown and gray caddisflies.

But the most impressive fly hatching now is a large black stonefly #10-3X long and it is relished by the trout. These large early black stoneflies really get the attention of the larger trout even though they are not as prolific as the smaller stoneflies. They like to splat down onto the river and that's the best way I can describe their activity. It sounds like a large raindrop or hailstone splattering onto the surface water. These large stoneflies then jettison their eggs using this collision of themselves with the water to break the eggs loose. On slow sections of the streams you can actually watch the bright yellow egg sacs sinking to the bottom. Some of these flies may drift on the surface for awhile, twitching as they die and enticing trout to surface rise for them. Most get sucked under water due to the collision and an observant angler can watch them struggling and working their wings underwater, which also attracts trout. Others who were unsuccessful jettisoning their egg sac will actively dive and swim to the bottom of the stream to lay their eggs on rocks or sunken logs.

The Mashpee River. It is the most natural river on Cape Cod with much of it unchanged since the time of Daniel Webster.

These large stoneflies give the angler an opportunity for moving and catching the larger trout present in the river. The most successful pattern has been a large traditional Black Gnat tied with a black chenille body, pale duck wings, black beard hackle and a yellow chenille egg sac on a wet #10-3X long hook. When you spot a surface-feeding or swirling trout during this hatch, it is probably one of the trophy trout in these waters (12"plus). Try him with a drifting, large, wet Black Gnat egg sac and allow it to move and swing through where you believe him to be. Often you will be met with an arm wrenching take. Tie up some large down wing patterns using pale, dun, mink tail hair with a black fur body and dun colored hackle on a long-shank, dry fly hook if you wish to tease these trout on the surface. A two-fly setup works well on such trout. In fact, I don't know why we fail to use more of this. Put your wet Black Gnat egg sac on the point and tie your dry fly as a dropper. Often, when a trout misses the dry fly you will take him on the wet fly and vice versa. This two-fly, wet/dry setup covers both the surface and subsurface preference feeders.

Don't worry about movement of your flies as long as you are not excessive. These trout are conditioned to take food that moves. They are feeding on baitfish, elvers, swimming nymphs, emerging caddis, and darting shrimps, so movement attracts them. In March, I have fished this little known hatch in year-round trout rivers successfully on New York's Battenkill, Connecticut's Farmington, the Chattahoochee in Georgia, as well as these Cape Cod rivers. Look for this hatching and trout feeding activity into mid-April.

Traditional patterns work well on the other stonefly and caddis hatches also. The brown and red stoneflies of March are well imitated by the time honored Coachmans: the royal, the white wing, and the lead wing. The egg sacs of these brown and red flies are more a greenish tint than yellow. I find the Royal Coachman the most overall effective pattern during these hatches, particularly when they are egg laying. When wet the Royal Coachman's rear sac represents a greenish egg sac. Its front thorax and the red body, when wet, appear brownish-maroon. The red hackle points mimic the leg color of many flies, and the white wings are close to the off white wings of the insects. I believe that the proven effectiveness of the wet Royal Coachman, for over 100 years, is due to the fact that it suggests so many different egg laying and hatching stoneflies, caddis, and mayflies throughout the season that have reddish brown bodies, egg sacs, and light colored wings, particularly drowned spinners. The lead wing and white wing Coachman do well tied with a gold tinsel tag, again suggesting an egg sac. The golden pheasant tippets as tails have been much maligned by some of our best fishing authors, but I find them useful during actual hatches. Look in backwater eddies during and after hatches of stoneflies, caddis, and mayflies, and you will find these insects struggling to rid themselves of their nymph shucks. These shucks are most often amber to reddish brown with dark contrasting markings, and trail the hatching insect bodies. The golden pheasant tippets tied as tails on such patterns is not an affectation but a perfect suggestion of such naturals.

You will generally have to tie your own patterns with egg sacs, tinsel tags, and golden pheasant tippets, as, again, fly shops and their catalogs have abandoned these successful patterns as being old fashioned when, in fact, they often will out fish the more modern patterns consistently. Besides, they look better in your fly box.

There is another effective pattern for these stoneflies, particularly the drowning ones. It is a modified version of a combination of the Hornberg and the traditional English pattern named the Mallard & Silver. I have named my version the Lasko Herring Fry, as it is immensely successful from June through December, whenever herring fry migrate down our rivers to the sea. It is made up of an all-silver, tinsel body, sparse, mallard flank feather wings tied on the sides, and jungle cock eyes, and finished with a sparse, soft, grizzly, hackle collar. Many of the stoneflies, when they collide with the surface water, are coated with miniature air bubbles and, as the light of the sun reflects against them, their bodies sparkle like tinsel. This pattern has proved successful on sunny, bright days during these stonefly spinner egg sac falls.

As the month draws to a close, we find wood ducks, snipe, and woodcock returning to our little valleys and pairing up to mate. Quail begin calling bob-white and wild turkeys are clucking on the ridges, while male ruffed grouse are heard drumming in the woods. There is a large, three-foot diameter tree down across a favored pool on the Mashpee River where I have heard ruffed grouse drumming and found their droppings but have never seen the birds. However, this past year I heard the drumming and stealthily peered around a bend to find a male and a female grouse sitting on this log over the river peering back at me. Within seconds they flushed simultaneously, one going right and the other left. I felt like such an intruder and interloper to their courtship that I sheepishly backed away, stopped fishing, and headed for home, although I still had fishing time left.

Near the end of March, we are getting the occasional day of 65 degrees and once the waters hit 50 degrees on the rivers we begin seeing Leptophlebia—the Early Black Quill (actually a dark-reddish mahogany color-bodied, dark-winged mayfly #12) heralding that the mayfly season has begun. Both rivers are so full of food that these trout are as fat, or fatter, than trout you will find in other rivers in June.

And then the scouts make their appearance. These are adult herring in from the sea, called scouts because they are solitary and are a preview to the thousands of adult herring that will arrive in April, at times filling our little rivers bank to bank with their presence. With these scouts arrive the heron and osprey preparing for a three-month feeding frenzy on adult herring. Until the herring arrive they will satisfy themselves on our unsuspecting trout, who have flourished without these predators since November.

Small shrubs and bushes along the stream banks are spouting new green leaves while the oaks and maples stand gray as November, yet their buds are swelling every day in preparation for April.

APRIL

April may arrive with warm 60 degree sunny weather or blast us with a northeaster dumping 18" of snow. Over the past decade, I have experienced both on April Fool's Day. But Spring is in charge now and the sun shines longer daily, tilting the equation of light and dark into the favor of daylight. Any snowfall is temporary and disappears quickly with warm southern winds under the equinox's more direct rays of sun.

Grouse are drumming tirelessly up and down our river valleys and we smile at the good population of surviving males that have made it through winter and predators. At dusk we witness the mating dances of newly arrived woodcock and snipe as they twitter away with their high, spiral acrobatics and hear the music of air whistling through their primary feathers. Wood ducks are migrating through our little valleys daily. Some settle on our ponds to raise their broods while others continue on to Northern New England and Canada for their summer family homes. The returning songbirds, along with our year-round residents, are mating, making nests, and incubating eggs. Their singing brings the woods alive in full symphony before sunrise. We find quail sneaking away from us along the trails in pairs of two, and not in their coveys, in search of privacy for lovemaking. The sea ducks, buffleheads, mergansers, canvasbacks, and bluebills have already left for the Arctic to mate and raise their families.

River bank grasses are growing inches overnight, showing brilliant green shoots rising above the tan-brown, matted vegetation of winter. The maple trees are budding and their young tiny green leaves and red flowerets appear hanging over the rivers, already providing hiding places for hatching insects and light shade for our trout. Wild apple, crab-apple, cherry, dogwood, and shadbush are blossoming now. It seems that every day a new wildflower appears: coltsfoot, violets, primrose, forget-me-nots, and trillium. The high bush blueberry shrubs burst with flowers that will become the fruit we snack on streamside come August. The oaks still stand bare and winter-like, although closer examination shows their buds are swelling rapidly even though their leaves won't pop open until mid-May. The river water temperatures now nudge beyond the 50-degree mark on fair days and we note the watercress beds are enlarging, turning brilliantly green with fresh growth. Green aquatic weeds of every type begin to appear under water, so small that we are not wholly aware of their annual regeneration and yet, in just three months, we will need to trim the lower sections of the Quashnet River.

Baitfish of all types—shiners, sculpins, dace, and sticklebacks—are seen mating in the shallows among the water weeds and hiding there along with trout fry, elvers, shrimp, and damsel and dragonfly nymphs, as they all pursue the continuously hatching, smaller midge larva and pupa.

Large 18- to 24-inch suckers appear from nowhere and we watch intently as the large females mate with several males at a time. Where do these suckers come from? We do not find them in our rivers the rest of the year. In recent years, studies have been undertaken in Scandinavia and the British Isles indicating that fish such as trout, needing moving water to spawn, will actually use the outlets in a form of reverse migration when occupying a lake without inlets. Could that be the answer to this mystery? And do our sea run brook trout use reverse migration from Johns Pond on the Quashnet and Mashpee-Wakeby Lake on the Mashpee to accomplish the same thing as these suckers? Future studies may hold the answers to these questions.

We spy pods of brook lamprey eels just 6 to 8 inches in length. It is another species we never see the rest of the year. We watch a half-dozen working together, picking up small stones and gravel with their suction mouths and dropping these bits a foot away until they have cleared a smooth, sandy bottom depression in the streambed about 8 inches in diameter. Then suddenly, seemingly out of nowhere they are joined by dozens more. They all tangle together rolling about in the depression on the stream bottom like an anchored ball of loose twine. After 10 minutes of such frolic they drop away one by one and all disappear. I have noted that they pick the same spawning sites every April and have begun to look for their activity. They are relished by the trout during this season; we find our brookies spitting up these tiny eels as we release them. We also note their outline in the trout's stomach walls and can feel their presence. I have yet to find a definite scar on one of our trout from one of these brook lampreys, although in high summer I do often find blood suckers and leeches attached to the fins of our trout.

But the overwhelming migrants in our little rivers now are the 12- to 16-inch adult herring on their annual runs to the headwater lakes to spawn. The arrival of these herring is the most important event for the survival of our trout. Their herring fry offspring will provide a nearly constant food source for our trout from June to December and at times during these seven months they are the only substantial food source available. Without the adult runs upriver and the subsequent herring fry running back to the sea, our trout would not feed as well nor could our little rivers sustain their healthy trout populations. As these adult herring enter the rivers by the thousands, they become the main prey for the osprey and the heron cushioning their potentially devastating predation on our smaller trout population.

At times there are so many adult herring in our rivers one could walk across stream on their backs. Osprey and herons satiate their appetites leaving, first, piles of herring heads and then piles of dead unconsumed herring as they kill far more than they can consume. Predators are always practicing their art and continue to do so even when hunger is no longer an incentive.

In addition to being a buffer between our trout and the predation of osprey and heron, these adult herring protect our trout in another way. Sea run brook trout run in from the bays and estuaries interspersed within these herring runs. It makes sense. There is safety in numbers and what better way for our small trout populations to avoid predation while running upriver than under the cover of these massive, adult herring runs. A native American Wampanoag confirmed this phenomena when I happened upon him legally netting adult herring. I asked him if he ever netted trout accidently while fishing for herring. He nodded and pointed to a trout cruising upriver with a pod of herring as we spoke. Since that time, I have often observed brook trout swimming upriver with the adult herring. As these herring runs peak in May, we find more trout in the river. In the ocean, saltwater bays, and estuaries, water temperatures are warming and the adult herring bring in the large striped bass and bluefish who will prey on our trout as well as herring. These herring runs are a signal to our trout to enter the cooler waters of our little rivers, avoid the predation by the striped bass and bluefish, use the cover of the many herring to avoid the osprey and heron, and find their special summer hiding places in the river. Our little brook trout caught in May, fresh in from saltwater, often show fresh wounds from attacks by bass and bluefish.

The insect hatches are profuse now. The black, brown and red stoneflies are still hatching, along with wide varieties of gray and brown caddis. All the midges continue to appear, as well as the pesky, biting black fly. Fortunately this cursed biting fly of the north country does not appear in great numbers here, but after a few itchy bites we are certain to carry our insect repellent in our vests. The early black quill mayfly (actually a dark, reddish mahogany-brown body with dark blue dun wings) is a good mouthful for our trout in sizes #10 and #12. They are mixed in with the profuse hatches of the smaller early blue quills in size #16 (also actually mahogany-bodied), and the lesser hatches of the small quill gordons, size #16 and smaller than its north country cousins. Although these and other mayfly hatches are heavy on the Mashpee, they are less so on the Quashnet due to the horrific environmental damages done to the Quashnet by the cranberry growers prior to the 1960s. These hatches have been returning to the Quashnet in limited numbers in recent years, due to the tireless 50-year work of Trout Unlimited volunteers. In recent years, I have experienced wonderful April and May hatches of the early blue (mahogany) quills on the Quashnet, enjoying the pleasant early season dry fly-fishing these hatches create. Caddis larva drift in the rivers prior to hatching and have a fondness for our breathable new wader materials; they are often seen attached to our waders when leaving the river. It is a good harbinger to determine what color caddis hatches to expect in the coming days, be they gray, brown, tan, or green. It is the daffodil and the forsythia, however, that signify the coming of the prime mayfly hatch of the season—the heavy hatches of Hendricksons. Their eagerly awaited arrival signals the beginning of the best dry fly-fishing months. Although these hatches are heavy on the Mashpee, in recent years they can be found hatching intermittently in the upper wooded valley of the Quashnet as its mayfly populations continue their slow recovery.

I have found Hendricksons hatching as early as the first week of April on the Mashpee, a full month before they appear on the Farmington in Connecticut, the Battenkill in Vermont, or the Westfield in the Berkshires. This hatch is so prolific on the Mashpee and so long in duration (lasting until mid-May) that the trout focus their feeding on these flies and are seemingly oblivious to the thousands of adult herring passing by. Because of the character of the Mashpee, upstream dry fly-fishing is difficult, so the downstream dry fly method is an extremely useful tactic.

The Pheasant Tail Nymph, tied using pale orange silk, works well before the insects hatch, but the wet standard Hendrickson, with its tan body, wood duck flank wing, and soft dun hackle legs, generally is more productive. I have enjoyed mind-blowing days on the Mashpee with this 100-year-old classic pattern. And I have had similar good fortune on the Farmington, Esopus, and Schoharie. Like other classic wet fly patterns you probably will not find them in fly shops or catalogs and will have to tie them yourself. The standard dry fly pattern the Light Hendrickson works well, but an even better pattern substitutes dun hackle tip wings for the wood duck flank. I have proven this pattern's success on the picky trout of the Battenkill. One of my favorite methods of fishing this hatch is tying a classic wet Hendrickson on point with a dry Light Hendrickson as a dropper. You will take more trout on the wet fly, but the rises to the dry fly are very exciting. This is a terrific setup for downstream fly-fishing and often you will be rewarded with two trout on at once!

The Hendrickson spinner falls occur nearly every day and the hour of their mating and egg laying is a condition of water temperature, water level, barometric pressure, precipitation, approaching weather fronts, and wind directions. For instance, if there is a calm, warm morning before a late-day storm, expect heavy activity. It is the same if the weather is calm in the evening with a storm coming in the morning. It is important to be prepared for these spinner falls at any time of the day and not just at 6:00 PM, as so many of the books tell us. Forget those full spent wing patterns you see in all the fly shops and catalogs. Instead tie the standard Red Quill with dun hackle point tips for daylight and the old Iron Blue Dun with hackle points for evening fishing.

The majority of the Hendrickson spinners are taken by the trout (and this goes for all rivers in the Northeast) when the wings are upright—not flush to the surface! All trout are more interested in taking a live insect than a dead one, and the upright wings signify life to a trout. This holds true whether one is fishing the Mashpee or the Battenkill. Save your flush floating spinner patterns for hours after the spinner fall for feeding trout taking the dead leftovers. And observe if they may be taking what I call the one wing spinner—a Hendrickson rolled over in the current with its two wings stuck together as one. If you see this on the water merely cut off one of the wings leaving a stub on your flush-floating, winged spinner, fishing it with one wing and a little support stub.

In the falling light of evening during the Hendrickson spinner falls, I like to fish the old Iron Blue Dun with hackle point-tipped wings. It works better in the late evening than the Red Quill, because, I believe, the trout see the silhouette of its thorax against the fading light, which makes this pattern so distinctive. This pattern has been so successful for me that I have even impressed some of the old sages on the Battenkill. On the Mashpee, during late evening Hendrickson spinner falls, I like to tie a wet Lady Beaverkill with egg sac or a wet Royal Coachman on the point with the dry Iron Blue Dun as a dropper. I believe the trout see the wet Royal Coachman as a spinner with an egg sac against the light pattern. With these patterns, you will make some impressive catches in late evening during a spinner fall.

Again, in our race for modern patterns, we have overlooked the upright-winged pattern for spinners and the traditional wet fly for hatching nymphs or drowned spinners. Try these suggestions and I am sure you will improve your success with the Hendrickson hatch wherever you fish. Our fishing is so good in April, once the Hendricksons begin hatching, that we hardly realize when the month ends and May has begun.

MAY

May 1st is the usual starting date for fly-fishers here in the Northeast. From New York and across New England, it is the time of the first heavy hatches of mayflies on our famous rivers. The Beaverkill in the Catskills, the Farmington in Connecticut, the Battenkill in Vermont, and the Westfield in the Berkshires come alive now, with good hatches of Hendricksons, Gordon quills, blue-wing olives, and early blue quill mayflies joining the growing hatches of caddis and stoneflies.

Fly-fishers descend on these rivers and occupy pool after favorite pool, often hogging sections from other anglers. They beat the water to a froth with their pent up anxieties, generally having last fly-fished for trout the summer before.

But here on the Quashnet and Mashpee we have fly-fished steadily every month since last September and we feel no such pressure. We have caught enough trout in this new season since January that we have no need to push ourselves or rush our fishing. We can take things in stride and take time to enjoy all the beauties that nature and the rivers have to offer besides just catching trout.

Hendricksons are peaking in their hatching cycle on the Mashpee River now, while solid hatches of caddis and stoneflies continue to hatch and fill the niche on the mayfly-depleted Quashnet. The Quashnet surprises us with good hatches of the smaller blue wing olives and blue quill mayflies in the absence of Hendricksons. Air temperatures are improving daily as we experience some of the most pleasant spring weather of 50 to 75 degree days. Our water temperatures now remain above 50 degrees even on rainy, cloudy, chilly days, on its way to peaking at 60 degrees by month end.

Mixed in with and between the heavy hatches of Hendricksons on the Mashpee are hatches of black quills, blue quills, blue-winged olives, brown & red stoneflies, and tan, brown, and green caddis. The higher water temperatures speed up the trout's metabolism and we find them feeding voraciously from morning to night. At mid-month a small, light Hendrickson begins hatching and, even though the larger Hendrickson spinner falls will continue for several days, we know this greatest of mayfly hatches is over for another year.

Memories of Hendricksons are always bittersweet for me, as they remind me of my late fly-fishing friend of 25 years Ernie Long, who will no longer join me. Ernie, 30 years my senior, and I made it a point that no matter where I lived—Boston, Hartford, New York, Atlanta or Cape Cod—we would manage to fish together some time during the Hendrickson season on the Battenkill in Vermont. We lost Ernie one Christmas and I have missed seeing him cast his 7'6" Orvis bamboo Battenkill Midge rod, offering nymph, dry fly, wet fly, and spinner patterns to feeding trout at Hendrickson time.

We do need to exercise caution now with the warmer weather. Both river valleys are infested with ticks carrying lyme disease and other parasites. It's important to wear a large brimmed hat and turtleneck or other high-collared shirt. You will need to cover your face, neck, ears, and wrists generously with insect repellent. At home, run your clothing through a dryer after a day fishing to kill any hidden ticks. Pesky black flies will remind you of the need for insect repellent, which will also ward off mosquitoes that are known carriers of a wide variety of viral diseases and infections. I find pipe smoke also helps to keep them away. I have also deterred their biting through a shirt by wearing two shirts. It seems they are able to pierce their proboscis through one shirt layer but not two!

Yet, as we lament the passing of the Hendricksons after mid-month, we are met with the hatching of the even larger #10 March browns! The Pheasant Tail Nymph and the classic March Brown Wet fly are excellent for fishing wet while the Art Flick dry fly is the perfect adult imitation. Use an upright-winged, hackle tip Red Quill for its spinner, which is known as the Great Red Spinner. Jim Leisenring's wet fly, the Great Red Spinner, is good for fishing a wet drowned spinner. The grey fox follows the March brown hatch and smaller patterns #12 of the aforementioned patterns are just the ticket!

Our days have grown so long now that we find ourselves able to fish from 5:00 AM to 9:00 PM or any part thereof; we seem to move trout no matter what time we make for the stream. As May progresses, grey foxes, light cahills, and pale sulphurs hatch along with the sporadic March browns, and all the classic wet and dry fly patterns work well, even though the trout remain focused on the larger March browns.

At mid-month we notice the oak trees have finally opened their leaves, which appear to double their size every few days. By month's end the forests in our little valleys are so flush with vegetation that many pockets and pools are tree-shaded and will see little sunlight until autumn.

All through the first half of May we observed adult herring running heavily up our rivers in pods of 100 or more but by mid-month we find pods of 50 or more running downstream heading back to the sea. These were the early spawners who completed their activity in Johns Pond and Mashpee-Wakeby Lake and are now rushing back to the sea for safety and deeper water, away from the relentless attacks of osprey and heron. Waiting for them at sea, however, are millions of bluefish and striped bass, whose sustenance is the same adult herring that are swimming past and often bouncing off our wader legs as we move upriver. In departing, the adult herring do our rivers and our trout one last favor. A sticky brown algae has formed on the riverbed rock and gravel bottom under the direct, warm sun of April. That algae is now broken up by the action of the tails and fins of the herring and the currents wash it away, cleansing the river bottoms.

The fickle weather of early May leaves us by the third week, giving way to mostly sunny, pleasant days with air temperatures in the high 70s and river temperatures peaking around 60 daily. We discard our fleece under-wader pants. Our chamois shirts are packed away in favor of light cotton. Our waxed cotton hat is tucked away in our vest pouch, reserved for rain and replaced with a light cool cotton one.

Then Memorial Day is upon us and another May draws to a close as we welcome Summer.

Chapter Nine

SUMMER

JUNE

It can be said that May lets the fly-fisher have the cake and eat it too. Then June is the icing on the cake!

On the Quashnet, June means the arrival of the almost daily hatches of the summer blue quills, blue duns, blue-winged olives, and speckle-winged quills. At last we can enjoy daily dry fly-fishing activity in the classic upstream method along the lower Quashnet River, from Martin Road all the way to second sluice.

The blue-winged olives have various shades of olive bodies as duns and turn into amber-colored bodies as spinners. They hatch from morning to late afternoon and provide evening spinner falls. The blue quills, blue duns, and speckle-winged quills all have various shades of blue dun wings and gray bodies both as duns and spinners, while some spinners have mahogany-colored bodies. These blue-winged olives and blue quills are a great summer hatch on the Quashnet and, although they last through September, June is their heaviest hatching period.

These flies are generally size #16 and #18, and hackle tip, winged patterns with matching colored bodies or quill bodies are excellent. Be prepared with olive colored bodies for the blue-winged olive and quill bodies for the gray colored species. A simple pheasant tail nymph works for the nymph and the old classic English duck quill-winged wet flies—blue-winged olive, Greenwell's Glory, Blue Dun, and Blue Quill—work well for hatching nymphs and drowned duns and spinners. In fact, look to the British patterns for use during these hatches. The English have the greatest experiences fishing these hatches on their chalkstreams and their knowledge will serve you well on the weedy, spring-fed, chalkstream-like lower sections of the Quashnet. The Red Quill pattern with upright blue dun hackle tip points (British or American) works well on the mahogany-colored spinners. The spinner of the blue-winged olive body is an amber-orange color and the age-old British patterns—Orange quill, Ginger Quill and Sherry Spinner—are excellent matches to the blue-winged olive spinner falls. Again, you may generally leave your flush floating, spent wing spinner patterns in the box. These mating spinners fall to the river with upright wings, so pale blue hackle tip wings, tied upright, work best on these placid waters. An exception to this is that, if you are fishing at sunrise after the evening spinner fall the night before, you may find trout feeding on left over spinners that are dead and flush floating and that pattern is most appropriate.

Also hatching daily on the Quashnet are damsel and dragon flies along with intermittent hatches of Tan & Brown Caddis. I am not fond of the damsels and dragons when they are feeding on these insects, but accept the fact that these voracious feeders also eliminate every mosquito they encounter. At times the trout will rise to the damsel flies, particularly when they are laying eggs on the weedy aquatic plants in the river, and a damsel dry pattern will work.

Purple loosestrife and tall meadow grass overhang the summer, weedy Quashnet near First Sluice. The bank edges are good places to pitch tiny dry fly and floating terrestrial patterns. Trout will be found in the shady places.

The Mashpee River explodes now with mayfly hatches of grey fox, light cahill, pale sulphur, yellow drake, blue-winged olive, blue quill, yellow & green stonefly, tan & brown caddis, and damsel & dragon fly. The lower river also experiences a week long massive hatch of alder flies. There is so much going on at the Mashpee in June that, often, you don't know what fly to use.

June is usually a sunny pleasant weather month with air temperatures ranging from 70 to 90 degrees and water temperatures of 58 to 65 degrees. On hot breezy afternoons half-inch carpenter ants fall like raindrops on the heavily wooded Mashpee and along the wooded upper sections of the Quashnet. Dry or wet black ant imitations, along with the old standby Royal Coachman (suggests a-winged ant), work well during this period. And the ant activity is usually during the hottest time of day, when the mayfly and caddisfly activity is less active. This heavy ant activity signals the beginning of terrestrial dry fly-fishing, particularly along the lower Quashnet with beetles, leafhoppers, ants, inchworms, and their appropriate patterns.

On calm, humid mornings and evenings, mosquitoes may hatch in such large numbers as to drive you from the stream. Be prepared, especially now, due to the reports of their carrying various diseases, with insect repellent, double layer shirts, pipe, and hat.

Adult herring are still running upriver, but many more are now running downstream and back to sea. We find a fair number of dead adult herring in our rivers from the stress of spawning. These fish provide still another benefit to our trout. Their decomposing bodies provide food for all the underwater creatures, maintaining a rich food chain to sustain our trout.

We observe two-and-one-half-inch baitfish guarding their half-inch offspring in the shallows from the remaining trout fry, who have already grown to three-inch fry on the rich food life of the rivers. Sucker fry are available to our trout in huge numbers along with tadpoles. Streamer patterns and woolly buggers work well between hatches.

It is now light from 4:00 AM to nearly 10:00 PM, providing 18 hours for fishing as we enter the longest days of the year. Trout populations are peaking as they migrate upriver to cooler water from the warming estuaries and bays, escaping the growing populations of predatory bluefish and striped bass. We find it difficult to choose between the Quashnet or the Mashpee for fishing, like someone in love with two people. Do we go to the Quashnet to fish the blue-winged olive hatch? If so, will we miss the Grey Fox hatch on the Mashpee? It's a dilemma, but, with 18 hours of fishing potential, we can more easily divide attention between the two rivers than at any other time of year.

With so much insect activity, oddly enough, we still may encounter a fishless day. It is then that we are jolted back to the reality that, when trout do not want to play or feed, neither we nor our fly patterns are infallible, and our trout are not always cooperative. Nature still shows us humility, and, after having been so successful in our fishing, we need the reminder that we can not win every time out. But we know the trout are here and that, if we are fishless today, we can return tomorrow or the next day and succeed.

All the summer birds are here and they seemingly are all in contests to see who sings the most frequently and the loudest. Quail are constantly calling up their chicks and calling to their covey. With luck we may encounter quail or grouse with their chicks. About once a year I encounter a Ruffed Grouse with chicks who plays the broken wing act. When I refused to fall for it one year and stood still, I spotted the walnut-sized chicks frozen in place among the ground vegetation. The hen grouse, disturbed that I wasn't fooled by her antics, then charged me, coming within three feet hissing at me while standing on her toes and menacingly flapping her wings. Frankly, it was an unnerving experience. Once she saw I was neither leaving or advancing she stalked away, keeping one eye on me while she clucked lightly, calling her chicks as they scurried to her side. She and her brood then quietly slipped away into the underbrush.

Flowers are everywhere—laurel, rhododendron, rose, beach plum, starflower, Indian pipe, and lady slipper. June is a month when I get so distracted by nature that, at times, I miss hooking and lose a good fish because I am looking at birds, flowers, or insects. But no matter, there is always another trout to catch and, after all, it is summer. We have time to daydream whenever we want.

Then, one day, we spot the first pods of one inch long herring fry making their way downriver. This is cause for joy. We know the adults have had a successful spawning season. We are comforted that for the next six months these fry will provide a constant supply of food for our trout, regardless of the lack of insect activity, which is already waning and telling us it is high summer and July has arrived.

JULY

This is the month when heavy pods of herring fry begin their runs to the sea on both the Mashpee and Quashnet. When in the mood, the trout stuff themselves on the one-inch herring fry and, at such times, you may move 20, 30, or more trout on the right day using appropriate herring fry streamer patterns. But there are other times, more frequently, when you arrive at the river to find thousands of herring fry running and you are unable to interest a trout. It is because the trout are stuffed and temporarily not feeding. Then it is best to work the known holding lies, methodically moving some and catching a few trout by changing to bright streamers like the Chief Needahbah or a Mickey Finn, showing them something different to strike either out of anger or in the spirit of play. Sometimes a tiny wet Royal Coachman, fished slowly, works best. Or you may do well enough by fishing dry flies upstream and interest those trout who want a little something more, but not another herring fry. They may be acting like we do after a heavy meal, simply looking for a light dessert. Usually we are appealing to the trout's hunger, but at times like these we can appeal to their mind, using other tactics to get them to take a fly. Often, when trout have had their fill and you can move them, their takes may be quite subtle, so be sure your hook points are as sharp as they can be.

Two-inch herring fry schooling on a Quashnet backwater in July, preparing for their run downriver to the estuary and the sea.

Then there are those sunny, hot, humid, warm water days when nothing works or those showery thunderstorm days when the trout hide and refuse to feed. At such times, I take up some stream improvement work. Aquatic water weed always needs cutting or pulling on the Quashnet in July, so this is a good time to go at it. Both rivers need pools, pockets, and holding lies cleared of downed trees, limbs, and debris, which keep falling after windy days and thunderstorms, so this activity can be coordinated with the dead and slack trout-taking times. Be sure to check in with Trout Unlimited about areas and the type of work required before commencing. It would be good for you to spend some time with TU work parties on the rivers so you learn what work is appropriate. The British hire river keepers to maintain their waters, especially on their weedy, eroding chalk streams. We need to do the same habitat work to nurture our trout and also to more fully enjoy our fishing. There is no greater satisfaction for me than to have cleared out an unusable, destroyed, past holding lie one week and then to find it occupied a week later by several trout. It is a real pleasure to make such small accomplishments. And yet, if we each take a half hour from our fishing outing each time out, in the course of the season we will have helped to increase the trout populations in our rivers ten to twenty percent with just these simple maintenance efforts. Usually the only tools required are your two hands.

On the Quashnet, blue-winged olives, *callibaetis*, and the little blue quills may hatch at any time day or evening, particularly on cloudy days. Along with their spinner falls, this provides dry fly opportunities for the patient, observant angler. Caddis species are smaller now, usually #16 and #18, in shades from cream to tan and light brown, and generally hatch in early morning or evening. Ants continue to fall into the rivers along with inchworms, beetles, and leafhoppers of varied descriptions and sizes. A variety of black gnats may appear at any time, usually sized #16. Winged ants also may appear at any time, but particularly on hot, windy, sunny afternoons, in black, red, mahogany, or cinnamon, though black is the predominant color. Although an upright-winged dry fly pattern is the match, a dry Royal Coachman works well. Hold one against the sun and you will see that it has a silhouette suggesting a winged ant. In fact, this is a good, searching, dry fly summer pattern in #14 or #16 when you do not see anything hatching or rising.

On the Mashpee River, in addition to all the above, you will also find hatches of the pale little cahills, little red quills, pale olives, yellow drakes, and a variety of summer stoneflies.

All the spring flowers have disappeared now, but we find the large honeysuckle in bloom. The continuously blooming white, blue, and pink, wild rugosa roses appeal to both our sight and smell as we sense their perfumed aroma along the river banks. Although we try not to notice, we are increasingly aware of many ground shrub leaves turning red and orange—harbingers of the autumn season even though summer has just begun.

Our rivers are shrinking now, becoming low and clear. It becomes harder to interest many of our old friends in our flies; they were more gullible earlier in the season. The trout seem to get lazy and either ignore our flies altogether or drift along with them disdaining them in the end. We hope and pray for rain. We look for a soft, gentle "Irish" rain to disguise our presence along the stream and camouflage our casting. We want a slow-rising river that only slightly discolors, with gently rising water running cooler to activate our trout to take more aggressively. But nature seldom provides such cooperation. Instead, more often we get no rain and a state of drought or sudden heavy rains that discolor the river, putting off the trout until it clears. The Mashpee seldom discolors for more than a day, although I have seen the Quashnet run a muddy, murky brown for several days and, when finally clearing, get hit with another heavy rain discoloring it once again.

The ospreys and herons continue to work over the river and its inhabitants. When an osprey flies by with a two-foot eel or a large sucker, I feel no remorse. When I see them go by holding twelve-inch trout (trophies for our little rivers), I yell and shake my fist to no avail, but I feel better for it. Single adult herring, along with pairs of two or three, are still seen in the river. They are stragglers from the spring runs, returning cautiously to the sea. Often you will spot injured ones, victims of a heron's beak or an osprey's claw, and you know that fish is marked and eventual easy prey. Osprey- and heron-injured trout show up in every fifth trout I catch and release. With my ratio of trout-moved to trout-hooked-and-released at fifty percent, this means that ten percent of our surviving July trout have been attacked and injured. In the shrunken rivers of summer, predatory herons and ospreys reduce the trout population more than we know.

Every April through October, several herons and ospreys take up residence on both our little rivers. By summer the adult herring are nearly gone. So we can deduce that they are eating good proportions of trout and not just eels, suckers, and field mice. Often I will come upon a heron or an osprey near what I knew to be good trout holding lies and their heavy white wash is indicative of their stay there. And I find no trout left in those lies. Two pairs each have taken up homes each year on the Mashpee and the Quashnet over the last decade. The effects of DDT are waning and the successful breeding and increased populations of these magnificent, deadly predatory birds are good news for the environment. However, we should stop and consider just how many breeding pairs the ecosystem can handle rather than thoughtlessly building more artificial nest sites that may now be unnecessary and may even lead to potential overpopulation. The more we interfere with the natural environment, the more we need to look at the bigger picture and not just osprey and heron versus trout, or coyotes and hawks versus grouse, woodcock, and quail, but look to maintain a balance. All creatures deserve the right to populate and exist, but let us look toward maintaining a proper balance in our ecology rather than artificially preferring one species over another just because it may be more politically correct at a given moment.

And so, we, as lazily as our trout, spend July fishing our rivers. We enjoy a few successful days using our herring fry patterns, while we watch for a hatch of mayfly or caddis that will bring up the trout so we can take a few on the surface with our dry flies. We spend more time cutting weed, knowing that if we don't, there will be little fishable water left on the Quashnet by August. We keep open the pockets and pools that get filled with debris, while we enjoy the pleasant days of summer with its chilly mornings and cooling evenings paralleling its often hot, sunny, humid afternoons.

We hardly notice that each day we are losing a minute or two of daylight as the long days seduce us into believing this pleasant weather will never end.

Then, seemingly in the blink of an eye, it is August.

AUGUST

I am never conscious of the arrival of August until I have to write a date with the number eight preceding it. There is not much difference in the last seven days of July and the first seven days of August. Yet we instinctively know that August means the summer is more than half gone. Along the rivers, we know it is August as the green grasses of spring and early summer have turned to a tan honey brown, never to see green again until next spring. Purple loosestrife and orange spotted touch-me-nots greet us along the river edges and, if we wait long enough, silently and patiently watching, we may see a red throated hummingbird or a ruffed grouse feeding on the spotted orange flowers.

Most days and nights find the air hot, heavy, and humid, despite strong southwest sea breezes of 10 to 20 mph. We relish a few days of cool Canadian air that punches out the humidity, transforming the gray, hazy skies to crystal blue and carrying light, dry, sunny breezes from the north. When the heat and humidity are upon us, we wear the lightest cotton shirts and even fish in our tee shirts. The cooler intervals send us back to our chamois shirts in early morning and late evening. These cool dry winds of the north have started their fight with the hot humid winds of the south to see who will gain the upper hand. However, after a brief retreat, the south winds win each match.

Like the weather and ourselves, the trout are lazy in the humidity and rambunctious on the cooler days. Along the Mashpee, we stop and pick wild blueberries to have with our tea breaks. But by the third week of August the blueberries are gone.

The herring fry keep migrating down both rivers from the lakes of their birth, but they are not seen every day. We look for a good rain to flush them down from the ponds in rising water and for the same rising water to bring some estuary trout upriver. These fresh run brook trout are silver blue and quite aggressive when they first enter the upper river holding areas and you will find sea lice on some of them. In a matter of days they assume the regular colors of a brook trout, as if they changed clothes. The occasional sea run brown trout is silvery when he enters, before turning an uninspiring rusty brown. A 13" fish, brook or brown, is a giant as the trout continue to average 7" to 8" in length. Once in the rivers for a few days they become as lazy as us.

Damsel and dragon flies continue to hatch on both rivers but are heaviest on the Quashnet and there are always a few of the swimming nymphs crunching in the trout's extended bellies as we release them. There are still blue-winged olives and the little blue quill species hatching on the Quashnet and Mashpee, but not in the numbers of June and July. A wide variety of smallish #16 and # 18 tan to brown caddis continue hatching on the rivers providing dry fly-fishing to rising trout when encountered. The Mashpee still has small light cahills hatching while the Quashnet may show us hatches of *callibaetis*, the speckled-winged quill. Be alert to the hatching of little red quills. Trout respond well to the time-honored Adams dry fly in #16 and #18 for all these mayfly and caddisfly August hatches.

One of the most interesting hatches that begins now is a #16 little black caddis that is on the water before sunrise and at sunset. It avoids sunlight and only gives us about a half hour of fishing in early morning and late evening. This hatch continues to grow in quantity throughout August and peaks in September. The larger trout will actually prepare for this hatch by taking up position in the main feeding lies from which they were absent all day. In the darkness before sunrise and in the fading light of evening, they know they are temporarily safe from the osprey and herons. This little black caddis looks like the early black caddis we see in April and May, and is a harbinger of cooler weather to come in September.

Evenings on the Mashpee will also create hatches of the white mayfly—*euphoron*, creamy tan nymphs, White Miller wet flies, and cream Cahills all work for this late evening hatch at dusk. Black Gnats of a wide variety of species can appear at any time and can save a day of dry fly-fishing on the entire Quashnet system. They are usually smallish, about a #16. The classic Black Gnat dry fly works well for these two-winged, land-based insects, as well for the aforementioned Little Black Caddis.

However, August is truly the month of the terrestrial. Mayfly and caddis hatches may be sparse, hit-or-miss propositions, while the terrestrials are available to our trout all day long. Ants, wasps, bees, inchworms, leafhoppers, early small grasshoppers, crickets, moths, and beetles (who do have wings and fly) either fall, fly, or get blown into the rivers all day. When hatches are non-existent, fishing dry terrestrial patterns on the lower Quashnet or Mashpee usually works, as the trout have been well conditioned to take surface food. The exception is when our trout are focused on feeding on migrating herring fry. Sometimes there are so many different insects hatching, terrestrial activity, and herring fry runs, that each trout acts individually, taking a particular insect while letting others go by. That is when it may be best just to go with an Adams or a Royal Coachman dry fly, as these patterns have the characteristics of many different insect species. You will save yourself from making excessive fly changes and pass up the pickier trout as there is another around the next bend that will probably take your fly.

August is the peak of the small fly, dry fly-fisher's season. We ignore the heat and humidity. We keep working at our stream maintenance in between hatches and enjoy high summer. And then one morning, without warning, the air is cold and almost frost-like. We shoulder into our waders and realize that a chamois shirt will not be enough, so we search for our wool fisherman's sweater and pull it on. We are comforted that we put on slacks instead of shorts as we wade into cool water and are pleased that we brought along two hot thermoses of tea. We look past the swamp maples at dawn, which are turning red and orange. On the river, a cool northern breeze makes your wet fingers feel numb after releasing a few trout and you begin to wonder where you packed away your fishing mitts and your wool Irish fishing cap?

But moments later the sun rises and the south winds return. You are warmed again and you shed the wool fishing sweater. Your thoughts return to summer, even though the blueberries are gone and Labor Day awaits around the next bend in the river.

Chapter Ten

AUTUMN

SEPTEMBER

Here on Cape Cod, Labor Day weekend means the beginning of autumn even though its calendar arrival may be three weeks away. And it is not only because Labor Day sends all the summer tourists back to school, college, and work. Every year, on or about Labor Day, autumn sends in a cold chilly blast of air across this little island-peninsula, which is so powerful that everyone knows we will not see 80 degree temperatures again for some time. These autumn winds from Canada no longer play with the summer wind of August and then retreat. These winds are here to stay. When the breezes from the south collide with the winds from the north, the south winds give way and retreat.

Overnight temperatures plunge to the forties and most days are hard pressed to reach seventy degrees. The annual Atlantic Coastal runs of hurricanes and tropical storms blow by, usually in a northeasterly direction, kept off our coastline by the northern winds. Fortunately we usually only receive their leading edges of heavy rains. Such rains swell the rivers, raising them 3" to 6" in a matter of hours. Herring fry leave the lakes, flushed downriver to the sea by the thousands. When the rains subside, we are met with clear blue lively skies and bright sunshine, and enjoy days of the most pleasant weather.

The Quashnet River Trail in October

And yet, some inner clock tells us that we can no longer take the time to do things that the warm days of summer allowed. No matter how hard we try to maintain the slow easy pace of summer, we find our actions take on more speedy behaviors. We find ourselves moving more quickly and are less interested in taking time just to sit at the beach. No, now we must be accomplishing something. We can no longer afford to waste any time.

On the rivers, we watch the swamp maples going bare, their shed leaves beginning to cloak the bottom of the stream, even though the sugar maples are just beginning to turn and the oaks are still green. The sun rises later in the morning and sets before 7:00 PM. We are losing minutes of daylight each day. The cotton fishing shirt is discarded and the turtleneck and chamois shirts we had set aside in May once again become our fishing uniform of the day. On wet chilly days we reach for our waxed cotton Barbour coats, realizing too late that they need reproofing, as the rainwater seeps through to our shoulders and arms.

Our trout are feeding heavily on the late-running herring fry which have grown in the lakes to 2″ to 2-1/2″ long, doubling their size of summer. Trout bellies bulge with them and our trout, after short feeding sessions, retreat to rest under some dark undercut bank. Our success in fishing streamers can be magnificent when the trout begin to feed, and totally unproductive when they cease. Our water temperatures now drop from the mid-sixties of August to the mid-fifties. Temperatures are reverting to those of late April and May. Our hatches too are more reminiscent of early spring. Blue-winged olives, pale olives, red quills, and blue quill hatches are heavier, but of short duration, as in springtime. Little dark stoneflies begin hatching, along with larger red sedges, on both of our rivers. The dry fly-fisher remains alert for these hatches and rising trout, which may occur at any time of day depending on conditions, but most generally are found between 11:00 AM and 3:00 PM as in spring.

Although ants, beetles, and other terrestrials are found on the water, September ushers in the grasshopper season. Starting small with a #14 simple Letort Hopper and gradually increasing to a #10 by month's end brings up good fish. But the largest, most consistent hatch now is the black caddis #14, found on our rivers every morning before the sun gets too high, and in late afternoon into evening wherever shadows fall across the water. Interested trout leap up out of the water, like jumping brook trout in Winslow Homer prints, impatient for the swarms of mating dark caddis to land on the water. Again these sedges are more the color of the early black caddis of spring, as nature reverses herself. A good, dry, dark dun or black caddis pattern works well in morning or evening, along with the upright-winged, traditional Black Gnat, if our trout have not been overindulging in herring fry. Often, impatient trout will leap into the swarms of caddis, knocking several onto the water surface, then making continuous, rapid rises to take the insects trapped in the surface. When you observe such behavior, pitch your fly immediately to the area and your pattern will disappear in a sudden taking swirl. This activity is usually made by larger trout.

As September days roll by, we seem to catch less trout, but they are fat and well developed—even the smaller parr-like trout. We see runs of 6″ elvers and 3″ brook lampreys schooling within the herring fry pods and running to the sea to complete their life cycles. We see, and sometimes are lucky to catch, the more sizeable trout, some so silvery blue that we know they are recent arrivals looking to find a mate and their ultimate spawning grounds of November. And, like the autumnal insect hatches similar to the spring season, we hear grouse drumming in September as if it were March or April again. It is another irony of this early autumn that mimics Spring. By month's end we recognize that we no longer see the osprey and heron and we are glad they have begun the journey that will take them south, some all the way to South America. It is nature's way of reducing predation on our soon-to-be vulnerable spawning trout.

We take our breaks with hot tea now. We no longer have any need for cool drinks as our long underwear and fleece pants go on under our waders. Waders that leak are no longer tolerated now, as they were in summer, and are quickly replaced. Terrestrials can be important if enough are on the surface and the trout have little other foods available during any given day or given time of day. It will pay off for you to continue carrying a wide range of these patterns as well as your artificial grasshoppers.

But our trout are becoming even more wary and cautious daily; with so much varied food available they can be as choosy as they wish. A week of warm weather may take our midday highs into the seventies and the summer-like sun lulls us into a temporary, but false, sense of security. But with fires on the hearth nearly every night and new deliveries of firewood requiring stacking, we cast a wary eye toward the later sunrises and earlier sunsets and the changing leaves, as we feel the even cooler air of October wafting down our necks.

OCTOBER

October comes in with cooler air temperatures of below 60 degrees; any day higher is an anomaly. Although on Cape Cod only a third of our trees are turned on October first, half will be bare and the rest turned to autumnal colors by the end of the month. The first week brings an early killing frost. As we leave footprints in the early morning ice-crystal grass and scrape ice from the windshield, we know autumn is in full bore with winter not far behind.

We find the thousands of spotted orange touch-me-nots along the river banks being voraciously consumed by the grouse and quail as we flush them while fishing. That first frost kills the flowers and lays the plants down. The observant angler knows a frost is coming when the flowers are nearly gone; the birds seem to be able to anticipate the frost that will kill these vitamin-enriched plants and flowers, so they eat them before it happens.

For the first time since April, air temperature highs are only in the 50s and water temps go as low as 46 degrees on cold cloudy days. Gone with the flowers are the honey bees who worked so feverishly all through September. As we fish through another harvest moon, we are subjected to several northeasters, those wind-driven, cold, wet rainstorms lasting three days, which, when repeated in January, become blizzards. The higher river waters now rip out and carry away weeds, easily cleansing the spawning gravel of both weed and silt. The weed weakens and rots as the storm waters carry it away. Whole sections of the rivers, where we labored long and hard in July and August cutting weed just to keep an open channel, are now cleared by nature in a matter of hours. Our little rivers, thus, have more open areas to fish, and our leaders and flies get less hung up in trailing weeds.

The trout, however, retreat to under the banks and submerged roots and logs in the absence of weed cover. They are harder to coax out of these lairs with a dry fly, unless a hatch is on and they are visibly feeding. Cloudy, overcast, warmer days seem to be the best in bringing trout to the surface on the dry fly. The black midges of winter begin hatching now in a range of sizes from #14 to #28. Although light in quantity compared to their heavy density of their winter hatches to come, such appearances may trigger trout feeding behavior. Through mid-month, the grasshoppers are important but following a succession of frosts they are gone for another year. The little red sedge continues to hatch, but it is the large or Giant Red Sedge, a #10 or #12 caddis, that brings up the trout. This strong heavy hatch may be seen on the rivers any day into December.

October is a good month for the large #12 black-winged ants on warm sunny days. Along the slow water sections of the Quashnet, these winged ant hatches may be heavy. You will need to watch the feeding trout closely to ascertain what stage of ant individual trout may be taking. Some only want an ant as it raises its low-slung wings upward, so you will need an upright-winged ant pattern to interest such fish. Others will focus on the dead or dying, fully flat, flush, spent-winged ant spinners and you will need that pattern. A Royal Coachman wet fly will connect with below-surface feeders looking for drowned, winged ants.

Every day, Canada geese are honking overhead, passing by on their migration to Chesapeake Bay and beyond. Our resident snipe and woodcock move on, but we are met with new arrivals fluttering up in our faces as we stalk our way fishing along the river banks. The early season puddle ducks show up on their southward journey—wood ducks, widgeon, green- and blue-winged teal, and mallards—in ever-increasing numbers. Our waterfowl and upland bird hunting seasons open the third week of October, as the earlier turned leaves fall, assisted by the northeastern wind and rainstorms. The woods are more open, as are the banks of our rivers.

Now the fly-fisher must be more cautious, certain that his attire blends into the woods background so as to be undetected by the trout. The fly-fisher moves slowly as he fishes his herring fry imitations and bright attracter streamers as the mood fits the day, the trout, and the angler. One marvels at the daily, seemingly continuous runs of herring fry, who have now reached the size of 3" or more. We hook and catch leaves frequently and they often ruin either our cast, drift, or retrieve, resulting in putting down the very trout we were trying to entice. We move some really good fish and catch a few red-sided, slab-shaped, hook-jawed males and lighter colored, small-headed, football-sized females, fattened by both the food available and their ever-swelling egg sacs, nearly ready for the spawning gravel.

Sunrise is at 7:00 AM and it is dark by 6:00 PM. The colder days dictate that, along with a thermos of hot tea, we carry in our fishing bags our wool fisherman's mitts and our waxed cotton hood, in order to fish through the often cold, rainy, wet weather that comes between the sunny, clear, blue-sky days.

We find more trout parr and smolts in the rivers now and wonder where they spent the summer. Was it in the upper lakes or the estuary? Or have they simply grown larger, unnoticed, on the vast numbers of insect and baitfish? We come across fat, well conditioned brook trout holding in open water, no longer fearing the departed osprey and heron, finning comfortably, unperturbed, sharing their holding pocket with herring fry, trout parr and smolts, and even other trout. Such trout rarely feed now, as they have other things on their minds. As we stalk our way along the rivers, we look for past spawning sites and silently retreat when we find trout there once again procreating.

Such findings convince us to resist wading and fishing. And even though a few sunny days may warm us, the spawning trout and bare trees signal that we have now entered November.

NOVEMBER

When Indian summer days linger into November, the first week is not much different from October. But we are on borrowed time now. Frosts are nearly every day and any lingering oak or beech leaves now turn brown. The last of the leaves descend to the bank and the river for a final drift and float. By Veteran's Day we know it is November, as we are subjected to snow flurries and even an overnight dusting that leaves a white crust on our neatly stacked firewood.

November calls the outdoor sports person to many different paths: the water fowler to the swamp, marsh and estuary; the pheasant hunter to the fields; the grouse, quail, and woodcock shooter to the uplands. It finds me continually drawn to the moving waters of the Quashnet and the Mashpee and the wild little brook trout. But, like the trout, my interests are not just in the fishing.

Now a final survey can be made of all the previously known spawning sites, as we discover some new ones. In years past, one would find brown and brook trout using the same redds, which resulted in the sterile hybrid Tiger trout offspring. Since the end of the brown trout stockings in 1993, we no longer see such happenings and find all our spawning trout to be our beloved sea run brookies. I avoid wading and fishing half the Mashpee mileage and all of the upper Quashnet mileage, as these areas hold the spawning redds and their eggs that will hatch in winter and we must give them as much protection as possible and avoid disturbing them.

An 8" autumn brook trout caught and quickly released on the Mashpee River using a 6' French Pezon - Michel "Midget" rod with an Orvis CFO -1 Disc reel.

Herring fry continue to migrate downriver in smaller groups that move quickly to the sea, although you will not see such activity every day, as you had in early summer. The large Red Caddis continue to hatch on fair weather days and their patterns, along with our herring and streamer patterns, continue to be effective even though the water temperature is a steady 46 degrees and the highest daily air temperatures rarely exceed 50 degrees.

Juncos show up at our bird feeders and buffleheads drop in on our lower river estuaries both telling us of arctic weather approaching. By Thanksgiving the trees are bare. The winter sea ducks, mergansers, loons, bluebills, and brant geese arrive every day, adding to their flocks as they ready for their soon-to-be winter homes on Cape Cod Bay and Nantucket Sound. Our trout have completed their spawning cycle. The woodcock are no longer flushed along the river banks; the soil has frozen and they have migrated southward to the Gulf Coast States, where their long beaks can continue to probe soft soils for food. Ice forms on riverbank water-trailing grasses and branches. The river banks are hard frozen now and our feet are no longer comforted by soft earth.

We still manage to catch a few trout on our streamer and caddis patterns. We are pleased to see that, in spite of having spawned, our trout are healthy and continue to fatten up on the runs of herring fry and large caddis hatches. We love Thanksgiving when it arrives, and anticipate all the joys to come with the holiday season it ushers in.

And yet as we rest before our fading firelight we know the woodcock are gone and that our trout and our fishing will continue to diminish with the arrival of December.

DECEMBER

On warm days, December still provides fair fishing. Remnants of the herring fry runs are still available to the hungry, spawned-out trout, along with the year round baitfish supplies of shiners, horned pout, chub, sticklebacks, and sculpins. Black midges of all sizes hatch daily, as long as temperatures are above freezing, and the large Red Caddis still remain available. Heavy hatches of land-bred winter moths find their way onto the rivers and all these insects still provide some dry fly-fishing opportunities for the dedicated fly-fisher. We find that the sea run brook trout will still come to our flies.

But we find many pockets and pools seemingly devoid of trout and, although we live through this phenomenon every year, we still fear for our sea run brook trout. Have the bird, sea, or land predators drastically reduced their numbers to the point of no return? Has some man-made chemical pollutant migrated undetected into our rivers and killed our trout? Have they gone to sea? Have poachers taken our fish? Are they wintering over in the lakes or are they hibernating under the log embankments? Fishless hours create doubt, worry, and fear. Then suddenly we are rewarded by catching a few healthy brook trout and are finally reassured enough to climb from the river and take the trail back to our Jeep. As we get out of our waders, take off the wet, frozen, woolen fishing mitts, and pull off our sweaters and warm the vehicle, we think happy thoughts of the warmth to be enjoyed at our home fireside.

December weather can be 50 degrees, sunny, and fair, or bring below zero wind chills and snowy blizzards. Black ducks ride in ahead of the snowy cold arctic storms by the thousands, warning us of the frigid cold to come. Once the air temperature drops below 32 degrees, ice forms in your fly rod guides and your fishing is over until a few days of above freezing weather can be strung together. Due to the 50 degree spring waters constantly entering the rivers even in this cold, the waters almost never drop below 44 degrees. If you can catch the weather right, you will take trout on wet fly, streamer, and dry fly patterns. I have found pods of migrating herring fry as late as Christmas Day on the Quashnet, with trout chasing after them.

But nature's weather is undependable now. From the Solstice on December 21 through New Year's Day, unusually cold, snowy weather may arrive, so bitter cold that even hardy duck hunters retreat to their wood stoves to spend time repairing, carving, and painting decoys. Some fly-fishers decide to put away their rods and begin tying fly patterns for the next year. But for me neither the year nor the season is over yet. There are other rituals to perform.

Every year, on Christmas Eve, I place a special bamboo fly rod under the tree. It was a my dad's Christmas present in 1950. And when all is calm and quiet, and I am alone by the flickering fireside, I remove the rod from its tube and bag and joint it up and flex it, and memories flood back from that 1950 Christmas Eve, when I spied my dad doing the same at midnight with this very rod. A libation toast completes the ritual, and I tuck in for a long Christmas Eve's night.

But mild days bring us back to the river Christmas week, just to fish once more before the year is over. We want one more chance to see our trout as we hope for a hatch of fly. And we will do it even with a crunch of snow beneath our frozen, felt-soled wader boots and clumps of snow dropping from tree limbs and down our necks. And we hope for just a trout or two to cooperate. But if the trout do not come, it doesn't matter. We hear the birds that had gone silent in November begin to sing once again. Ancient man credited Solstice magic for the renewed singing and I concur. We know the spawning redds will soon be releasing trout fry and that the lives of our precious little brook trout have another chance of renewal and rebirth.

And then the day comes for that final ritual of the season and the year. New Years's Eve is usually so bitter cold that it is impossible to fish or do much outside, other then run for a few logs for the fire. Around midnight, I will review the year's season in my mind, including, perhaps, new insect hatches discovered, the largest trout seen or caught, the most effective fly patterns, the best hatch experienced, and maintenance work completed. Fishing friends who are no longer with us are remembered and toasted.

And then, just as the melancholy may be too much to bear, I realize that all it will take is some southern breezes in January and air temperatures above freezing and I will be back on my little rivers, bundled up to be sure, but fishing again for our lovely little sea run brook trout.

Joy overtakes me then. I realize that there is no end to our trout season here on Cape Cod. At the moment we think there is an end, there is instead a new beginning. Just as this season ends in an instant of time, the new season begins. Surely that is what this holiday season and the life of a fly-fisher is all about.

PART THREE:

THE FISHING

Donna Lasko, the author's wife, is swinging a wet fly through a Mashpee River run in late winter well protected in her waxed cotton Barbour coat, boot foot "wellies" and carrying a bag with a thermos of hot tea. The rod is a delicate 6'6" 1960 Orvis Flea.

Chapter Eleven

CLOTHING AND GEAR

Color

After many years of fishing these rivers, the trout have taught me how sensitive they are to movement and particularly to any bright color of the fly-fisher's clothing. These wild brook trout, since birth, are constantly attacked by kingfishers, osprey, herons, and fish-eating mergansers, so they are aware of any unnatural movement and flash of color coming from above the water's surface. When fishing these little rivers, as well as other little trout rivers anywhere, think background color, and, here on Cape Cod, think green. Always think darker greens such as forest green or hunters green as appropriate clothing. This goes for not only your shirt, tee shirt, and turtleneck, but your hat, fishing vest, and waders as well. A dark green shirt is a must but is of little value with a white tee shirt under it. The white flash will scare the trout. In cooler weather use a dark green turtleneck under your shirt.

Once I seemed to be scaring or worrying nearly every trout I approached, no matter how careful I tried to hide myself from them. After an hour of such frustration I broke from fishing for a tea break and, when looking at my hat on the ground beside me, the epiphany came. My dark green hat of three seasons had been faded by sun, wind, and rain and was now nearer to khaki in color than its original forest green. When I put it on a stream-side bush 75 feet away it stood out like a white flag against the green bank side foliage. The trout picked up the movement of the unnatural colored bright hat. It is not easy to find a good, dark green fishing hat in the bucket style, which I suggest as it will keep ticks and rain away, while a baseball-style cap will not. You may have to buy one of your choice and have it dyed dark green.

In recent years, fly-fishing vests have finally become available from most outfitters in choices of bone, khaki, pale green, and dark green. Buy the dark green vest and if you own a light-color vest, dye it dark green. Going fishing in these rivers with light-colored vests and clothing makes you just as visible to the trout as the British redcoats were in our forests to native Americans, militia, and frontiersmen during the colonial wars.

The Vest

Although one may avoid using a fly-fishing vest, it is foolish to do so, as they are immensely useful. A fully stocked vest keeps all your necessary accessories and gear in one package. On a few occasions in winter, I have ventured forth without my vest and invariably, no matter how well stocked I thought my pockets and shoulder bag were, I found myself always without an accessory or fly box that could have made my day more enjoyable and successful. My dark green fly-fishing vest is always fully stocked and hanging in our laundry room. When I am ready to go fishing, I just grab it and everything I need for an hour, a day, or a week is already there. Get the vest with the most pockets and go for the shorter wading length rather than the full length. This will save your fly boxes from getting wet when wading deep or fishing from a kneeling or crouching position. Also buy an oversized vest that will fit over bulky jackets beefed up by sweaters, etc., for use during cold, inclement weather.

My vest carries a lightweight hooded rain jacket and a waxed Barbour bucket hat in the back pouch along with a journal and pencil in a sealed waterproof bag. There are two pouches for reels and I carry a spare reel with a different colored line as well as a spare spool with a different style line. Every now and then a reel breaks down and a spare reel in your vest will save the day. If I am fishing a floating line, which is usually the case on these rivers, I always like to have an intermediate line on the spare spool to use in some deeper sections or pockets with streamers, nymphs, or wet flies should the opportunity present itself. Intermediate lines may also be dressed to float.

The inside upper pockets hold a stream thermometer, a magnifying glass, and a leader wallet stocked with leaders in a variety of lengths and tippet ends. Encountering a broken or failed leader several miles from the replacement in your car or, worse, many miles from home, will, at best, shorten or, at worst, ruin your fishing day. I have my fishing license laminated so when it gets wet it will not self-destruct and this is in a zipped, inside pocket as well. My lower inside pockets are partitioned for tippet spools and are filled accordingly. The large, zipped, inside pockets hold several boxes of flies.

The outside front of my vest has five hanging accessories. A tiny Swiss-style, two-inch flat pocket knife is on one zipper hold and an air temperature gauge is affixed to another. There are simply scores of uses for the little pocket knife, and the air temperature gauge allows me to record air temperatures in conjunction with stream temperatures, correlating the relationships of seasons, weather, baitfish activity, and insect hatches to trout behavior. Another zipper hold has a dark leather amadou patch for drying dry flies. Pinned to one top pocket is the all-purpose fly-fisher's black clipper and pinned to another is a black forceps; both are on retractable cords. A fly-fisher simply cannot live without the clipper, and the forceps are a must to perform proper release of your hooked trout. Both of these are in black as I found that the silver ones gave off too much sparkle, worrying the trout. Decades ago, one had to hide these formerly silver accessories in a pocket.

One upper, large front pocket holds a fly line cleaning kit, insect repellent, and a waterproof cell phone pouch. When I break for lunch or a tea break, it only takes a few minutes to stretch out your line and clean it. I find that by doing so, my casting improves along with the sensitive feel of a trout's take. It is surprising just how much unseen debris collects on our lines in just a few hours of fishing. The insect repellent is a must have. With disease-carrying mosquitoes and ticks, annoying, tiny, biting flies and spiders, and bees and wasps, you want always to have insect repellent. Since cell phones became popular, I often come across fly-fishers streamside with their phones going off or yelling for the other party to hear them. This is so disconcerting, I admonish them for it. After all, a major reason we go off to the woods fishing for trout is to seek solitude and to get away from noise and such things like phones. And, frankly, I don't want to hear you scolding a child, a wife, an employee, your attorney, stockbroker, or your tax accountant streamside, while I am trying to fly-fish for trout. Nor do I want to hear about your real estate negotiations or the status of your lawsuit. There is simply no place for this nonsense on our trout streams, beaches, or uplands. It is long overdue that such cell phone addicts stay away from such areas if that's what they intend. They have missed the point of why they fish for trout and they are totally inconsiderate of fellow fly-fishers who are out there to get away from such craziness. Enough said on this subject.

I have learned, however, the value of having a cell phone on your person. I certainly can excuse a medical professional or one experiencing a true emergency. I keep mine turned off. I can check it when I take a break for emergency messages and only make a call when absolutely necessary and away from others out of sight and sound. The real value of this apparatus, though, is if you or another are injured, lost, become ill, find someone poaching or performing illegal activity, or are concerned with your personal safety (such as times when I have felt threatened by a group of drunken beer partiers or arrived to find my vehicle broken into). It is important to be able to call appropriate authorities and family members. The cell phone is wonderful for personal safety and security and we should always have one with us. Just keep it turned off and only use it when absolutely necessary, always being mindful to preserve your fellow fly-fisher's peace, silence, and solitude.

My opposite, large, zippered pocket holds a cellophane bag of pipe tobacco, pipe, and lighter. I do not mean to disconcert you. We are all aware of the health dangers of tobacco. I am not a smoker. But there are times in the woods along these rivers that you will find yourself swarmed by biting mosquitoes. These mosquitoes may carry deadly diseases such as Eastern Equine virus and deaths are reported in Massachusetts every year. Although you are well prepared with your clothing and insect repellent (which by the way can cause skin cancer, but who would go out without it?), when they swarm, one may find that vulnerable area at your neckline, behind an ear, or under your wrist. I find that smoke is a terrific deterrent and my pipe and tobacco are reserved for such emergencies only. I find such moments usually occur just before sunrise, at sunset, or in those dead air periods between wind direction or weather front changes. Fortunately we are often saved by the appearance of insect feeding birds, dragonflies, damselflies, and, at sunset, bats, who are all capable of rapidly greatly diminishing the numbers of mosquitoes. The temporary, added protection of smoke will give you the additional protection needed. Many of our fly-fishing greats over the last hundred years, such as Robert Traver, author of *Anatomy of a Fisherman,* have written about the value of such smoke as a deterrent. The lighter allows you to start a fire in the event of an emergency such as hypothermia due to a wetting or becoming lost.

This large, zippered, upper pocket also holds a leather-covered, felt-page, fly wallet of soft hackle, wet fly patterns that have been developed over hundreds of years and made popular in recent decades by the writings of Ernest Schwiebert and Sylvester Nemes. Another sealed bag contains band aids, antiseptic cream, and paper tissue.

A small outer top pocket holds a three-inch fine jeweler's stone. It is the best sharpening stone made for fine fly hooks.

There are four large, lower, zippered pockets that hold separate fly boxes for wet flies, dry flies, streamers, nymphs, and terrestrials. Other smaller pockets on the front exterior hold small boxes of specific patterns, such as ants, jassids, beetles, and midges, in a variety of patterns and sizes. More information on fly patterns will follow. These smaller, specific pockets and boxes allow me to access just the fly patterns that are hatching and useful, instead of going into the large, zippered pockets and large fly boxes. A few other outer, small pockets will hold tippet spools of 4x, 5x, and 6x for easy access of these most utilized sizes.

This vest is always ready to go and filled with necessary flies and accessories for fishing these two rivers, and to fish for trout in my annual sojourns to the Battenkill and the rivers of the Catskills. At the same time, it is filled with necessary personal security and safety items for protection and, if needed, survival in the woods.

Chest waders

Chest waders are necessary to fish both rivers due to the depths encountered throughout the Quashnet and the pocket hole depths found on the Mashpee. There are many locations on the Quashnet that are six feet deep and others where soft boggy mud bottoms sink you a foot deeper. Some pockets on the Mashpee, particularly in periods of high water, are easily chest deep. Hip boots are simply too short. At times, in shallow sections, you will need to fish on your knees or crouching, so waders are the only choice no matter the river or section you are fishing.

Once again, dark green waders will blend with the coniferous background trees and shrubs year-round and with all foliage late spring to fall. It is getting harder to find dark green waders and, once again, the light colors available today are simply too worrisome to our cautious trout on these rivers. The lightweight breathable waders are the best and the most comfortable.

Waxed coats

Inclement weather and cold weather require special clothing, which I have written about in Part Two, but it bears repeating. I love the green, waxed cotton, Barbour coats. They are warm and, when properly maintained, effectively keep out water for an entire day. They allow one to fish through the wettest weather. After all, they were invented for fishing and hunting in Scotland, Ireland, Wales, and England due to their damp, cold climate, which is similar to Cape Cod. I own a wader jacket, a midsize length, and a long coat model, and they are simply invaluable. Although expensive, they are often available on sale and last a lifetime.

You can re-waxed them yourself or have it done professionally; a U.S. location is available for repairs and waxing. The coats are a good investment, with sales in second hand shops sometimes exceeding the price of an original. They are also acceptable throughout Europe as sophisticated fashion as well as sporting attire, and are becoming more acceptable as regular clothing here in America. You can wear them inside or outside your waders and, combined with long silk underwear, fleece pants, turtleneck, chamois shirt, and a wool Irish fishing sweater, you will be dry and toasty warm. Add a green Barbour choker scarf, to keep moisture from your neck from going down your back, a wool Irish Fishing bucket type hat, wool open fingertip fishing mitts and six-hour chemical pack hand warmers in your pockets, and you are ready for anything mother nature throws your way.

Fishing creels and trout priests

Fishing creels and trout priests are to be excluded as the Quashnet is catch-and-release fishing only and all trout caught in the Mashpee should be released or you may expect the fishing ghosts to descend upon you for retribution.

Shoulder bag

My final piece of recommended equipment is a shoulder bag. I have two different styles of bag that I use depending on circumstances. You guessed it. The bags and their shoulder straps are green! One is a waxed Barbour bag that will hold a quart thermos of tea, sandwiches (pheasant, venison, duck, or partridge preferred), apples, cheese, crusty French bread, a bottle of ale or wine, and a flask of one's favorite libation. The other is a smaller, insulated bag that will hold either two pints of tea or a single pint with room for muffins, bread, cheese, and fruit. The insulated bag is good to carry a cold beverage in warm weather with a small cold pack to keep your snack food chilled as well. Often my fishing is only for a few hours in the morning, the afternoon, or the evening, which may include a short tea break. The smaller insulated bag is the choice for these excursions, but if I am fishing for the day and lunch time leaves me far from my Jeep, then the larger bag is necessary. Use unbreakable stainless steel thermos bottles, as the glass-lined ones will invariably end up broken.

I have numerous favorite tea break and lunch spots along both rivers where I can rest, sort flies, clean my line, repair leaders, make journal notes and watch for insect hatches and rising trout. The shoulder bags and well stocked fishing vest help to provide the comforts for these tea and lunch streamside picnics deep into the woods, adding to the joy of a fishing day.

Lunch break two hours from the starting point on the Mashpee River. Today's menu-bread, cheddar cheese, apple, tea, ale and a libation just as Daniel Webster himself would have enjoyed. All was transported in a waxed, green Barbour shoulder bag.

Chapter Twelve

ROD, REEL, & LINE

Rods

I have used rods as long as 9 feet and as short as 5 feet, while fishing these little rivers. I have settled on a variety of rods that range from 5¾ feet to 7 feet for the most effective and efficient use for fishing these rivers. If I were limited to one rod, it would be a 6-footer, although you will do well with a 6¼- or a 6½-foot rod.

Due to brush hanging over banks, overhead tree limbs, and the narrow rivers, longer rods can result in frustration, with leaders and flies tangled in branches, lost flies, and, worse, a broken rod tip. On these rivers you are more likely fishing downstream with wet fly, nymph, or streamer the majority of your time. Casting is generally reduced to strip and drift, and short, low roll casts using a variety of retrieves.

At times certain openings will allow the traditional overhead cast, but this type of casting will be found mainly in the lower half of the Quashnet and the very lowest sections of the Mashpee. In these areas, a long rod may be utilized, but you will still do better with the shorter rod. Overhead casts in these lower sections, using long rods on windy days (usually the prevailing condition), will allow the wind to catch your line and leader, while with the shorter rod, your line and leader may be kept below the wind for more accurate casting. Even in these more open areas, short casts are recommended as the trout could be holding in so many areas that casting over an unseen trout will spoil your chances. Even though this type of casting lends itself well to upstream dry fly-fishing, which is effective on these lower river sections, casts should be relatively short and the shorter rod will deliver the needed short, accurate cast.

The shorter rod, particularly on the 75% of your fishing that is downstream, puts you closer to feeling the strike of the trout. More often they are not strikes at all, but merely gentle takes, holds, or nips, depending on the moods of the day and the trout. Less friction and the less line between the rod tip and your fly help you feel and hook the trout more easily than a longer rod. Remember, these trout generally are only 5″ to 9″ long with only the occasional 10- to 12-incher and the rare 14-inch trout, so they are small; the delicate, sensitive, short rod keeps you in closer touch with your line, fly, and the trout.

When fishing dry flies upstream in the heavily wooded Mashpee and the upper woodland section of the Quashnet, the short rod again is the best choice. The short rod enables you to cast under the canopy lacework of tree branches using overhead, sidearm, roll, wave, and bow-and-arrow casts to drop your dry fly in likely trout holding areas. And after fishing a woodland upstream section dry, you can go the other direction and fish back downstream wet, having the necessary sensitive feel without changing rods.

The author's favorite bamboo rods and reels for use on the Mashpee and Quashnet. Left to right: 6'6" Orvis Superfine, CFO-II; 7' Orvis 7/4, CFO-I Disc; 6' English Hardy, Hardy Featherweight; 6'9" Custom, Hardy Flyweight; 6' French Pezon-Michel Midget, CFO-1; 6' Custom, Orvis BBS-I; 5'9" Custom, BBS-I.

My collection includes 5½- and 5¾-foot custom bamboo Heddon rods that I converted from 9-foot, circa 1950, damaged rods. I have a 6-foot Pezon & Michel French-made bamboo and a 6-foot English Hardy bamboo. My two 6½-foot bamboo rods are Orvis superfine models made in the 1960s. My 7-foot model is a 1990s 3-piece Orvis bamboo Seven/Four. I also use a 6¾-foot, 3-piece bamboo rod that I converted from a circa 1940, damaged Montague rod. I do use my father's 7½-foot 1950 South Bend bamboo rod that I restored to honor him, mostly when fishing dry flies upstream on the more open lower Quashnet River.

All of these delicate, sensitive rods will fish three-weight or four-weight lines. My preferences when fishing these rivers are the 6-foot Hardy, the 6-foot Pezon & Michel, and the two 6½-foot Orvis Superfines. It is a pity that Orvis no longer makes these short, simple bamboo rods. At one time in the 1970s, before graphite entered the fly rod scene, Orvis made these impregnated bamboo models in lengths of 4¼ feet, 5 feet, 6 feet, 6½ feet, and 7 feet, with simple cork grips and sliding, simple cork reel seats. These were full to medium flex, sensitive, delicate rods perfectly suited to 3- and 4-weight lines and to small stream fly-fishing. I would hope that Orvis one day will return to making these models available at a reasonable price to the small stream flyfisher. Their sheer simplicity should allow production at affordable prices.

Line

I carry double-taper and weight-forward floating lines colored tan and green, and amber intermediate lines in 3-weight and 4-weight. I utilize the tan-colored lines from November to April, but once the foliage is fully out I switch to green colored lines. By June, both rivers are not only overhung with the green foliage of brush and trees, but their river beds are alive with a wide variety of aquatic plants. Much of this green underwater vegetation constantly breaks off and drifts by the trout. Drifting a green fly line from June to October causes less concern among the trout. The tan lines seem to blend in better during fall and winter. Lately, gray-colored trout lines are available, so I intend to use those in winter to match the gray background of the leafless trees. I find no need for sink tip or sinking lines for these rivers.

I have no choice, it seems, on the color of the amber intermediate lines, as that is all that seems to be available. They do remind me of the old original lines I began fly-fishing with as a boy, so I do enjoy using them now. The intermediate lines allow me to sink my line and flies to deeper levels, particularly when fishing the deeper holes and pockets using wet flies or streamers, whenever the trout are holding deep. I also like that, by dressing the intermediate line, it will float and I can fish it upstream using dry flies. Then, if I wish to fish wet downstream, I can do so without changing lines.

Avoid using the bright, garish orange and yellow lines as you will alert and scare the trout in the up-close-and-personal style of fishing these rivers require.

Reels

When it comes to reels choose the smallest, lightest, and most delicate reels you can find. Set your drag to its lightest possible setting. Although most trout will be small, there are many underwater obstacles on both banks as you fish these rivers and, whenever a trout gets hung up in them, your light drag will save you from a sudden break off of the fish. Also any trout of 9 inches or more, particularly a fresh sea run, will run line off your reel and the singing of the little reel will be music to your ears. The delicate setting of the drag will also assist you in not setting the hook too hard when you have a take, helping you hook more fish. In summer the trout most often will dive into weed beds and, with the light delicate reel, you will prevent break-offs and have a better opportunity to catch the trout and work the fish out of these weed beds.

If you fish these rivers long enough and diligently enough throughout the seasons, eventually you will hook a strong, fat, 12- to 14-inch monster trout (for these rivers) that will rapidly rip line from your reel and, again, the delicate drag will prevent an immediate break off. Such fish are strong and often uncontrollable. The light drag will allow the fish to run into weed, branch debris, and underwater obstacles without breaking off as long as you play the fish carefully. Lesser reels without a smooth, fine light drag system will simply will not protect as well.

I have a number of such small, delicate, lightweight, smooth drag system reels in my collection that accomplish this task well. My well-worn 1972 original 2½ inch, 2.75 oz., gray Orvis CFO II spring and pawl drag, now out of production, helped me land my two largest trout ever caught to date on the Quashnet River, both 14-inchers, along with many others in the 10- to 13-inch range from both the Quashnet and Mashpee. Again, please remember, that trout of this size are rare on these rivers. I usually have over 100 outings annually fishing for them, so I have many opportunities to catch such trout.

My 1960s Hardy Flyweight is a $2\frac{5}{8}$ inch, 3 oz. reel, also with a spring and pawl drag, that has seen extensive service on these rivers. Its drag is just a hair less delicate than the 1972 original CFO, but it has performed equally well. My 1960 Hardy $2\frac{7}{8}$-inch Featherweight has a spring and pawl drag system sensitivity nearly equal to its smaller brother and I use it on my dad's rod, as it was the reel of choice for rods of 7 feet or longer on our Catskill Rivers in the 1960s, prior to the release of the original Orvis CFOs in the early 1970s.

In recent years, I have added the newer Orvis Bronze CFO disc drag system reels to my collection. I have the CFO I disc drag which is a $2\frac{3}{4}$-inch diameter reel, weighing in at 3.6 ounces. This provides a smooth drag nearly equal to the original gray $2\frac{1}{2}$-inch CFO II, but holds more line and is more strongly constructed both in its frame and disc drag system. This reel lends itself to multiple uses on larger rivers, while maintaining delicacy for our little rivers. This sensitive delicate drag system is identical for its sister, which I have also acquired and used—the Orvis Bronzed CFO II, $2\frac{7}{8}$-inch diameter at 3.9 ounces. I also like using this reel on rods of 7 feet or more, and it, too, balances fine on my dad's $7\frac{1}{2}$-foot rod as well as my Orvis 7-foot rod Model Seven/Four. This is another beautiful series of reels made by Orvis in strength, form, style, and function, all perfect for fishing our little rivers.

These reels, be they by Hardy, Orvis, or other fine reel maker, are costly, but they will not only allow you to land fish that you would have lost, they will last a lifetime, as my heavily used Orvis and Hardy reels have proven to me over the past forty to fifty years. They continue to fish well with their drag systems sweetening over the years.

Leaders

When I began fly-fishing as a young boy, you either tied your own leaders or purchased hand-tied leaders. About 50 years ago, knotless, tapered leaders appeared on the market but initially their tapers were inconsistent and they simply did not cast as well, particularly during dry fly-fishing when we ask a great deal of our leaders. So we stayed with our hand-tied leaders well into the 1970s, fishing them happily. When I began fishing these little rivers twenty-seven years ago, I found that my hand-tied, knotted leaders simply picked up too much weed and caused trout to break me off too easily, with the multiple knots getting caught in weed beds and branch debris. Drifting weed and other small floating debris also accumulated at the multiple knots as one was drifting or retrieving line, spoiling the drift and retrieve and putting off trout that may have taken the fly.

This frustration taught me to take a good look at knotless, tapered leaders. To my satisfaction, I found they had greatly improved since those early 1950s and 1960s and continue to do so each year. Today one can find a wide range of knotless, tapered leaders that not only have appropriate tapers, but are lightly shaded to resist reflection and glare from light. This latter quality is of extreme importance in fishing these little rivers. You may have had the proper rod, reel, green line, and a great fly on, but a sparkling leader will chase every trout in the river away. But be cautious in purchasing your knotless leaders, as some brands still have too much sparkle in them on sunny days.

The tackle at work on the Quashnet

Just several years ago, the value of the little sensitive fly rod, equipped with darkly colored, 4-weight line, delicate drag system reel, and with a knotless, tapered leader, demonstrated itself in my successfully catching and releasing my largest sea run brook trout ever on the Quashnet River.

It was a sunny, warm August afternoon on the lower Quashnet and nothing was hatching. There were some tiny tan caddis on streamside foliage and the odd damsel fly about, but there was little on the water. Now and again a rise would appear and in observing the water surface I would find occasional beetles and ants, mostly black and of a smallish size 16. I began fishing from an area I call "Log Drop" because years ago cedar logs for constructing log hides were piled here. They are no longer there, but my journals have so many references to this area as "Log Drop" that I have kept the name. Once you enter the river here you are in waist- to chest-deep water for the duration. I was fishing dry fly upstream, using my old original Orvis 6½-foot Superfine bamboo rod (which was later to be named the "Flea" model), with a green, 3-weight, double-taper line on my little old original 2½-inch Gray Orvis CFO II reel. My leader was a knotless 7½-foot tapered to 6X.

I proceeded upriver at times fishing a tan GS caddis, a dry Adams, a Jassid, or my Winged Black Ant, all in size #16. My goal was to have a leisurely afternoon picking my way upriver approximately 1,000 yards to the old concrete sluice way which I call "First Sluice." The trout in this lower open area are extremely cautious on sunny days and were only slightly active this day. They were not in the usual feeding lanes and were difficult to coax out of their hiding places under eroded undercut banks, man-made log hides, or overhanging foliage holding areas. A pair of ospreys and a blue heron helped keep our trout in their protective hides. Without a good hatch to entice them into the open, I simply had to try all the known hiding areas. After three hours of fishing, I only managed a handful of 5- to 7-inch brookies. But I love upstream dry fly-fishing on the lower Quashnet and I was content enjoying the afternoon and having some top water action, releasing the highly colored little brook trout. By now the 59-degree water that was so refreshing when I entered the river three hours earlier, with the air temperature near 85 degrees, had begun to feel cold and I was getting chilled. The late afternoon falling sun was beginning to allow shade on parts of the river and my air temperature gauge registered 75 degrees which only added to my bodily chills.

Finally, "First Sluice" was in sight and I was looking forward to getting out of the water, drinking the hot tea, snacking on the scone in my shoulder bag, and, frankly, getting warm once again. "First Sluice" is my favorite spot for taking a lunch or tea break on the lower Quashnet. And it always holds trout either in its six-foot deep, twenty-foot long hole on the south side, in its twenty-foot long, four-foot deep sluiceway, or in the five-foot deep hole above it on its north side. There is also a twenty-foot long, four-foot deep log embankment hide above this on the north side. All this water holds trout, but, being a favorite fishing section for anglers, it also holds some of the wariest trout in the river. On arrival, one can stand, sit, or lean inside the old concrete dam after removing gear and get out of the water and warm up. From this vantage point within the old dam yet above the river, one can look for rising trout for fifty yards north or 15 yards south. It is a good place to observe hatches, baitfish, and trout activity while resting and breaking for lunch or tea.

First Sluice on the Quashnet River where the large brook trout was caught and released.

My fishing success has been mixed here. Mostly I move no trout or simply scare one or two from feeding. But I have caught and lost enough sizeable trout here that I always fish it well before taking a break or ending my fishing day.

As I approached the big hole on the south side of the sluice I made short casts along its edge and bank, then slowly up its center without moving a fish. Then I heard a muffled rise or splash somewhere up inside the sluice way. I waited many minutes and, just about ready to give up, I saw a rise up inside near the north side opening of the sluice. It was a trout feeding in a nearly impossible holding place to cast to. Three feet above the water's surface were four crossing rusting metal bars embedded in the concrete walls that connect the east and west side concrete walls of the sluice way. The trout could only be reached by casting over the bars the entire distance of the sluiceway with the fly landing several feet in front of the north side sluice entrance with enough loose leader to allow the fly to drift the four feet to the trout's location within the sluice way. The line and part of the leader would all be laying atop the rusting bars for the twenty feet while the rest of the line would be subject to the current pull in front of me as I stood nearly chest deep in the pool below the sluice. I would also have to speed up the line and shoot it forward as trees were too close behind me to get enough line out to reach the trout in a normal overhead cast. If I were able to get the cast and fly to the trout, I could easily get the leader or line hung up on the rusted bars and either get stuck on the bars or lack the tension to hook the trout if he took the fly.

I removed my shoulder bag and fishing vest. I knew they would only get wet as chances were good that I was about to go over my wader tops by just attempting to reach this trout. Luck was with me as the sluiceway was now in shade and a strong south to north wind began blowing at my back. The trout continued to rise sporadically and the wind was blowing both winged and regular black ants into the water as I observed them drifting by.

My first attempted cast only made it halfway up the sluice but the line and leader laid out perfectly over two crossing bars and a natural, drag-free float of my upright-winged black ant actually worked. I was just 10 to 15 feet short of the target. My next cast resulted in my backcast getting caught in the willow tree behind me. Luckily I was able to pull the little #16 winged black ant fly free without breaking it off. The trout rose again. With pin cherry and pine trees overhanging the east and west side of the sluiceway and willows behind me, I could not lengthen my cast. My only choice was to get closer by entering the depths of the deep hole. I did this slowly and shivered when the cold water went over my wader tops and seeped inside behind my tightened wader belt and down my pant legs. I was close enough now to just reach the trout with my cast, but I worried that maybe my movement had scared other trout up into the sluiceway, putting down my feeding trout. Thankfully, within minutes, he rose again in the same spot several feet inside the opening of the sluice and just inches from the west concrete wall.

My next cast was too far to the east side of the sluice and collapsed along its wall, as the line and leader brushed against all, landing over three of the crossing bars and behind the feeding trout. I checked fly and leader, sharpened the hook point, and applied a spot of mucilin paste to the fly to be certain it would float. The next cast was true, with the line and leader landing across all four crossing bars and the fly gently touching the water about four feet in front of the trout and the leader in the air, loosely hanging from the last bar. The tiny white wings of the ant cocked perfectly and it drifted drag-free to the trout. The fly disappeared with a gentle rise. I ever so gently tightened the line in fear of the leader or line catching on the bars, and suddenly there was a great splash and the rollover of a bright, orange-sided, male brook trout of great size. He immediately took off upriver, leaving the sluiceway and zipping line from the reel. The line rolled out across all four bars as he tore through the five-foot hole in front of the sluice and dove through weed and debris under the long log embankment above. Then he stopped running. I entered the sluice, passing the little rod over my head and over each crossing bar, worried that maybe he broke me off under the log hide.

When I finally had the rod free at the head of the sluice and had retrieved the 40 feet of line, I applied a little tension and felt the throbbing of the trout. Then he took off again, going upstream. Somehow he missed tangling my line on a log pillar, but now I could see that a fair amount of weed was hanging from the leader and near the jaw of the trout. He ripped more line from the reel, then decided he didn't like going upstream and turned, flying past me and carrying weed between leader and jaw. This time my fly line got caught around me as he ran back toward the sluiceway. I pulled the line over my head losing my hat (never found), turned, and reeled in the drifting line as fast as possible.

As soon as I felt tension again, I realized my trout was back in the sluiceway, wildly crossing it back and forth, and splashing as he went. Then he left the sluiceway, heading south into the six-foot deep, twenty-foot long pool pocket, and stripping line from the reel. Now I had to wade, crouching under the crossing logs with more river water filling my waders and the little rod bent over and throbbing, the reel singing. Below this pool was a 50-foot shallow run of only 12- to 24-inch water, full of weeds and downed tree branches, and I feared that, if the trout got into that mess, I would lose him for sure. I had to try to stop him.

I reeled in line and put pressure on the little rod. He held for a few seconds at the beginning of the weedy shallows before diving deep into the big hole pool.

Taking in line, I moved around the big hole and positioned myself at the head of the shallows to try to keep him from heading downstream and hold him in front of me in the deep hole. The trout made another run up into the sluiceway, but I was able to bring him back to the deep hole, putting as much strain on rod and leader as I dared. After circling the pool I was relieved that miraculously the weed on the leader was gone. It had come off during all his comings and goings.

I was calculating where and how to land this tireless brute. There was a graduated, brief piece of grassy bank just before the sluice on the west side. I began backing up toward it when he decided to run again, this time diving into weeds and branches on the east side of the pool. He was hung up. I crossed the pool and, in water up to my neck, bent over with my head under water and reached down the line and leader, breaking up branch debris and tearing weeds until he was freed. He took off again with new weed hanging from his jaw and leader. But this time he only kept circling the deep pool and when I tested him it appeared he was not going to run on me again. I beached the fat, highly colored male brook trout on the little grassy knoll and marked my rod. The little #16 ant was embedded in his lower jaw and it took my forceps to get it out. Then I immediately got him into the water, working his gills and after several minutes I felt his strength returning. When he was ready, he deliberately swam off into the deep hole depths and disappeared. My marked rod measured slightly over the 14-inch mark.

In reviewing the landing of this incredible trout on such a weedy little river, I realize that I had the help of angels and the support of the fishing gods that day. To begin with I had the benefit of shade and a good breeze at my back, both of which allowed me to make the complicated cast to the trout. The line and leader could have fouled on any of the crossing bars, but somehow did not. If the trout had kept running, I may have never been able to pass the rod over the crossing bars. The hook embedded itself into the thick jaw gristle and therefore did not pull out, while a lighter hooked trout would have easily pulled free. I was fortunate that the trout failed to break me off on any of a number of heavy underwater obstacles and several bouts with heavy weed hanging from the leader could have met with disaster. Luck was on my side with this fish.

However, it was the short rod that allowed me to make the cast, pass it over the bars, maneuver my way up and down the sluiceway and through bank side foliage, and reach into the weed beds. A longer rod would have been too cumbersome. The delicate reel allowed the trout to run all he wanted without creating enough tension to break the line. The light, 3-weight, double-taper line not only made the delicate cast possible, but lay lightly on the crossing bars so as to not get caught up. The knotless leader prevented heavier accumulations of weed that would have either broken the leader or so tangled it in obstacles that I would have lost the trout. And thank goodness I had the sense to sharpen that little hook before the last cast.

There was little skill on my part. All I did was react to what the trout was doing and follow him upstream and down. At the end of the day it was the angels, the tackle, and the trout's actions that combined to give me one of those rare angling experiences that will never be forgotten.

L.L. Bean, Orvis, Hardy, and other rod makers continue to create new shorter versions of modern material fly rods that should work well on these little rivers, even for a dedicated bamboo rod aficionado such as myself, and are worthy of use.

Chapter Thirteen

THE APPROACH

Small waters require an angler's humility, patience, and quietude. These are little rivers or, to some, little streams, so before you begin your actual fishing it is of utmost importance that you prepare yourself mentally and physically.

You have probably just left the modern, sped-up world of chaotic comings and goings and so you are a bit "sped-up" as well – more than you may think or wish to admit or even be aware. If you charge ahead into these waters with the same fast-paced, aggressive work- and life-style of your everyday living, you are destined for disaster.

Spider webs will sear and stick to our face. Minute red biting spiders will fall down inside your shirt collar. Black flies, mosquitoes, and no-see-ums will feast on your exposed flesh. Perspiration will burn your eyes and ticks will burrow into parts of your anatomy not fit to print here.

Tea break at the pedestrian foot bridge on the lower Mashpee River, just above the saltwater estuary. The rod is a 6' English Hardy "Blue Ridge" model.

Trout will see, hear, or feel your presence and disappear into their hides long before you or your flies reach their water. Your leader and flies will be constantly tangled in overhanging trees and bank side brush, causing them to break off. And worse, you may crack and ruin your rod tip on an overhanging limb. You will be constantly repairing your leader and tying on new flies, while under constant attack from the aforementioned biting insects. You will trip on sunken trees, slip on muddy or rocky bottoms, and inevitably take a fall and a wetting, hopefully without causing serious harm to your body. Wet, frustrated, and depressed, you will crash through the underbrush looking for a shortcut back to your car, ripping your waders on green briar, disturbing yellow jackets, bees, and wasps, and breathing in swarms of those biting insects, which will follow you back to your car.

There is nothing easy about fishing these little rivers. They are demanding and they take no prisoners. Trust me. I have experienced and suffered all of these indignities and worse. A positive, specific approach needs to be cultivated by the angler in order to fish these rivers successfully and enjoy the fishing day.

I begin adapting my mentality by sipping tea during my drive to the river and concentrating my mind on possible river conditions, weather, hatches, the mood of the day, and what moods I may expect from the trout. In this manner, I remove thoughts from my mind about modern life and focus on trout fishing. Still, even after a half century, the anticipation of actual fly-fishing for trout finds me nervous with excitement.

On arrival streamside, force yourself to slow down. When I sense I am on adrenaline overload or my bucket is full, the worst thing I can do is charge the river. Continue to clear your head and focus on the fishing by slowing down all your usual preparations. Take longer changing clothes, getting into your waders, and gearing up. A good procedure is to stretch your fly line and clean it. It will cast and handle better anyway and this well spent time slows you down. Be sure to put on a high-collar undershirt or turtleneck and cover all your exposed flesh well with insect repellent. Wear a bucket-style hat, which you can douse liberally, inside and out, with insect repellent. Do this right away and, if the insects are pesky, light up your pipe in self-defense, while you proceed with fly line cleaning and gearing up. Although tobacco use is no longer politically correct, I do not inhale, and there is nothing like pipe smoke to keep away disease-carrying insects. And I only use it in necessary emergencies. Mosquitoes, ticks, and spiders are known carriers of very serious diseases so beware and use whatever will keep you healthy.

I have found, as have many of the famous British and American fly-fishing authors over the last century, that this is the perfect time to drink more tea. This beverage has nerve calming enzymes that help to reduce tension and anxiety and will further relax your body and spirit during your gearing up activities, and, at the same time, keep your mind sharp. Three cups combined, on your drive and at streamside during gear up time, will set you just about right.

And what will be the choice of rod for today? It will be that sensitive little six-foot or six-and-a-half-foot rod fitted with a light, delicate reel, wound with a 3-weight tapered line and its attached knotless leader. Your fly choice will be determined based on the time of year, the time of day, hatches anticipated, and the manner in which you intend to be fishing, upstream or down, wet fly or dry fly. And don't forget that shoulder bag filled with beverages and food. Your fishing will take you a mile or more away from the car and food breaks will ensure a pleasurable day. Now you are ready to head for the river.

Walk slowly but deliberately down the path to the water's edge of the river section you have chosen and stop and observe before entering to fish. Look for insect and bird activity on the water. Search for nymph shucks on logs and rocks, and check under shrub leaves for insects that hatched earlier. Take the water temperature and note the air temperature. Drink in the air and the smells of nature around you, letting the river and woods absorb you. If the fly you tied on back at the car was inappropriate, now is the time to make the change.

With the proper fly on we are finally ready to enter the river. We will need to move slowly and cautiously. Unlike a larger river (where most of us should be quieter than we are) every little step here sends out crunching sounds in the gravel and ripples of water that can be easily detected by our trout. Fortunately our green shirt, hat, vest, waders, and shoulder bag all blend in with the trees around us, and we need to utilize every piece of screening foliage to hide our outline. Where the foliage temporarily opens up we need to fish from our knees or a crouching position. We need to use downed trees, overhanging brush, and limbs, along with the natural curves of the banks to hide ourselves from the view of the trout. We need to fish stealthily, with slow, stalking movements and, at times, remain heron-like if we are to succeed. We need to become a natural part of the entire river ecosystem around us or we will worry the trout. We need to limit waving and moving our rod unnecessarily, as we find sometimes even normal, natural movements will put down the trout. These trout usually don't care to move far from their chosen lies, so we need to fish all of the water: the head of a riffle, each side, the center, pocket holes, undercut, invisible holes under the banks, along and within weed beds, and all obstacles, such as fallen trees, underwater roots, and submerged rocks. The trout may be in different micro sections of the water we are fishing and if we are hurried in our approach we will either pass them by or chase them into other trout who, in turn, will scare away wildly, ruining our fishing of an entire run.

Every step we take may show movement to the trout, changes our cover, creates new angles of our drifts and retrieves, and provides new locations to place our fly, while possibly exposing our presence to the trout. We are neither kings nor bosses here. We must become one with the river to succeed. Exercise care, keep the rod low, stay hidden, move quietly, and accept the fact that we are one of many predators stalking our trout. Our trout have many tricks they use to avoid all their predators, including you and me.

Use the insect repellent periodically, take a tea and snack break when the need or opportunity presents, and stop worrying about trying to catch every trout in the river. Look for wild fruits, wild flowers, birds, hatching insects, and rare plants, and listen for the drumming of grouse and the screech of an osprey. There is a cornucopia of rewards awaiting one who fishes these rivers using patience and humility. Leave your ego back at the car.

After all, although we fish to catch trout, fishing these rivers is about so much more.

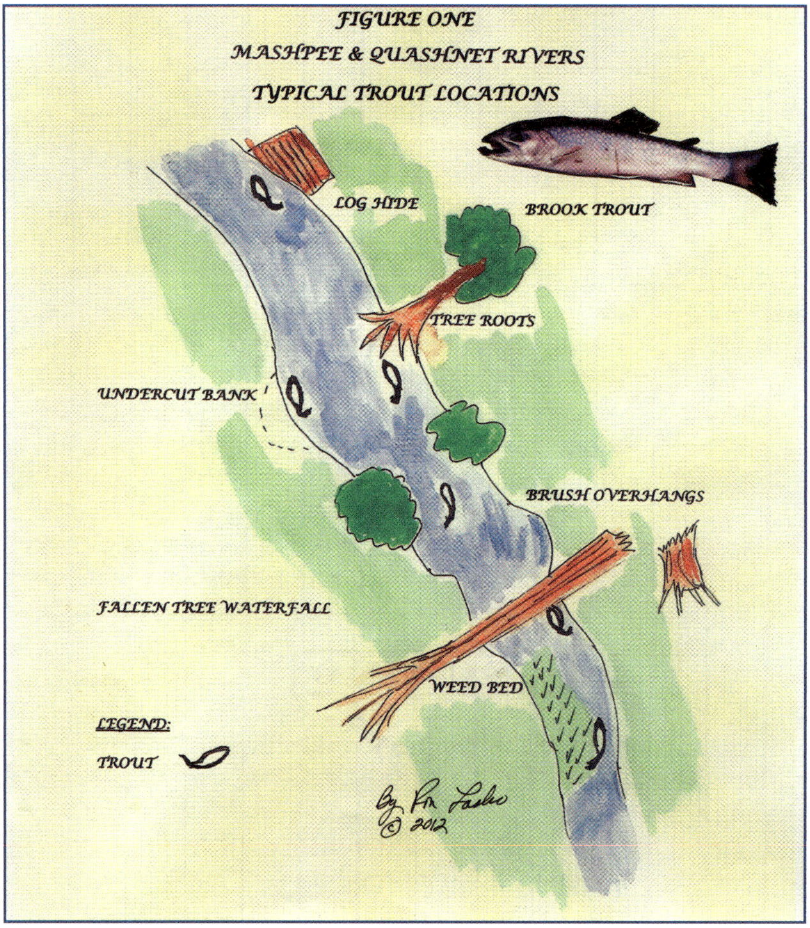

Chapter Fourteen

TACTICS

One may successfully approach the actual fishing for these trout by going upstream or downstream. Generally one fishes a dry fly when fishing upstream and a wet fly or streamer when fishing downstream, and for very good reasons, although one may fish a dry fly downstream and wet flies upstream with moderate success. Still, fishing dry flies up and wet flies down will generate the time-honored results that have been developed, experienced, and documented through centuries of fly-fishing and its literature.

Generally speaking, with some exceptions to this rule, anglers will move and catch more trout fishing wet than fishing dry. This may be disconcerting to many so called dry fly purists, but our success is due not to our fly-fishing techniques and abilities, but to the natural food available and the natural traits of a trout to protect itself. For most of the day and most of the year, the trout have simply more food available to them that is beneath the surface than drifting above or on the surface. And it is much safer for the trout's survival to be feeding below the surface the majority of its lifetime. And when the trout is not feeding, it is usually deep below the surface and, while in the depths, is more easily enticed to take a deeply sunk fly than to rise up to the surface to take a floating fly. This is the reality we face.

And I love upstream dry fly-fishing. Even when the season and the day may be only marginally suggestive of success, given the choice, I would choose upstream dry fly-fishing. I know, of course, that the stretch of river I am fishing may hold fifty trout and that my dry fly-fishing may only result in catching a half dozen, while if I was downstream wet fly-fishing I would probably move twenty or more and catch a dozen or so. Why be willing to only catch a half dozen trout fishing dry upstream when you could be fishing downstream wet and catch a dozen? It is the challenge of getting a trout, who is not inclined to rise to the surface, to come up from a four- or five-foot depth or out from under a safe hide, in spite of predatory danger to itself, and take your dry fly floating on the surface, especially when it doesn't really want to. It is to see your fly drifting quietly in a riffle or eddy one instant and in the next to see it disappear in a trout's rise. It is the feeling, as you tighten the line and gently set the hook, of life that is telegraphed through your rod and line to your fingertips that signifies to you that a trout is on. The adrenaline rush, the sheer joy, and the pride of accomplishment of the moment can only be appreciated by the upstream dry fly angler. The whole event takes place right in front of you and just often enough to keep you going at it like a golfer who hits the rare hole-in-one. Limited catches and fishless days can be all too common for the pure dry fly-fisher, but the mind-blowing days of scores of trout coming to one's flies keep the angler coming back. And the dry fly-fisher will experience those occasional days that no wet fly-fisher could ever come close to matching.

The wet fly angler may experience both fishless and limited catch days as well, but has so many more natural cause and effect circumstances throughout the entire year and many more tricks than the dry fly angler, which will usually result in some level of success no matter the conditions. Although the dry fly angler has a wide array of fly patterns and a range of techniques, he is limited compared to the wet fly-fisher. Wet flies, nymphs, soft hackles, streamers, and even sunken dry flies provide the wet fly-fisher with many more sunken patterns and ways of presenting them than exist in the dry fly-fisher's repertoire. And the wet fly-fisher will often succeed in the same stretch of river just fished unsuccessfully by the dry fly-fisher.

The truth is, that in this great sport of fly-fishing for trout, although we may choose to fish as dry fly or wet fly anglers, there is no need to limit oneself to one technique versus the other. We can do both. In fact, the very best anglers learn to utilize both the dry fly and wet fly patterns and techniques. They utilize them for success as nature dictates and allows, or they make deliberate decisions by choosing one method over the other on a particular day, river, or stretch of river. My personal experience is that I will often fish a section of river upstream using dry fly, have a lunch break, then fish the same section back downstream using a wet fly or streamer. Trout are individuals. Some are simply not oriented to surface activities while others are. By fishing a section of river both ways you will surprisingly discover different trout occupying different holding areas and will hook others that you had missed with a different method earlier. At times, I simply like to fish dry fly upstream until I drop and then head for home. Sometimes I am tired and the wet fly downstream approach is simply easier than pushing a dry fly and fighting currents upstream. It behooves the angler to learn both methods and all the fly patterns and techniques, in order to enjoy the limited amount of time that life allows us to fly-fish for trout. And then you can decide what method and tactic, wet or dry, suits your desire and gives you joy in any given season or time of day.

Wet fly and streamer fly-fishing is exciting, too. On these little rivers, your fly is generally just inches below the surface and you can follow it easily. One will often see the trout rush the fly or follow it, then take it, often with a splashy rise. The wet fly angler's composure is required if he is not to pull the fly away too fast and let the trout take the fly first, before gently setting the hook. By maintaining proper tension from the angler's hand through the line, along the rod, and on to the fly, the trout will hook itself. But I warn you, it is not easy to maintain coolness under pressure, particularly when a sizeable trout presents itself. Wet fly and streamer fishing, in addition to being a natural way of presenting insect and baitfish imitations, also locates trout holding lies that the dry fly angler may not be aware of. When located, such trout can be fished at a later date using the upstream dry fly methods.

So both forms of fly-fishing wet or dry are exciting and help create a fully developed fly-fisher.

The three diagrams in this chapter are of the same stretch of river. This portion of river is a combination of actual habitats found on both the Mashpee and Quashnet rivers. The first (Figure One, p. 80) shows the habitat of the river and where trout are likely to be found. There are undercut man-made log embankments, fallen trees, undercut banks, tree overhangs, bank side brush overhangs, waterfalls, boulder runs, weed beds, sunken tree trunks, underwater stone berms, and rooted tree pocket holes shown that all provide cover and habitat for our trout. Without these covers we would have few, if any, trout present. Most of these covers occur naturally, with the exception of the log embankment hides, which are man-made and designed to prevent erosion of the stream bank while providing overhead cover for the trout. These are found throughout the Quashnet river, having been installed since the 1960s by Trout Unlimited volunteers. You will find vestiges of these on the Mashpee River from over 100 years ago when they were installed by a private trout club. Much of the Quashnet habitat has been augmented or created by TU in an effort to reverse the mass destruction of the river by cranberry growers in the 19th and 20th century. Most of the Mashpee habitat is naturally created as the majority of the river was not subjected to past destruction.

Figure Two shows the same length of river being fished upstream with the dry fly, and Figure Three is the identical length of river, diagramming how a downstream wet fly-streamer fly-fisher would fish this river via cast, drift, and retrieve. The point of the diagrams is to show where the trout are generally holding and the ways they can be fished.

Now we will discuss the different specific casting, line handling, and retrieve methods for each type of fly-fishing.

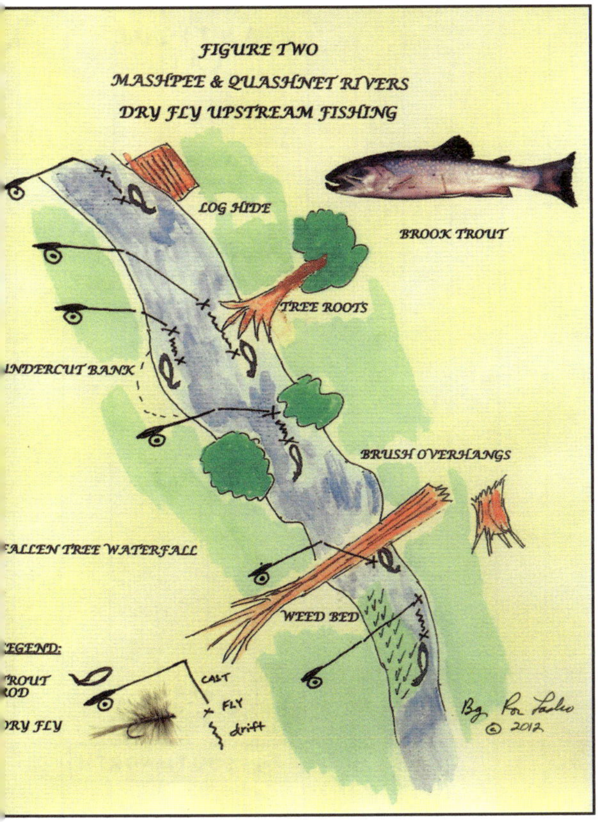

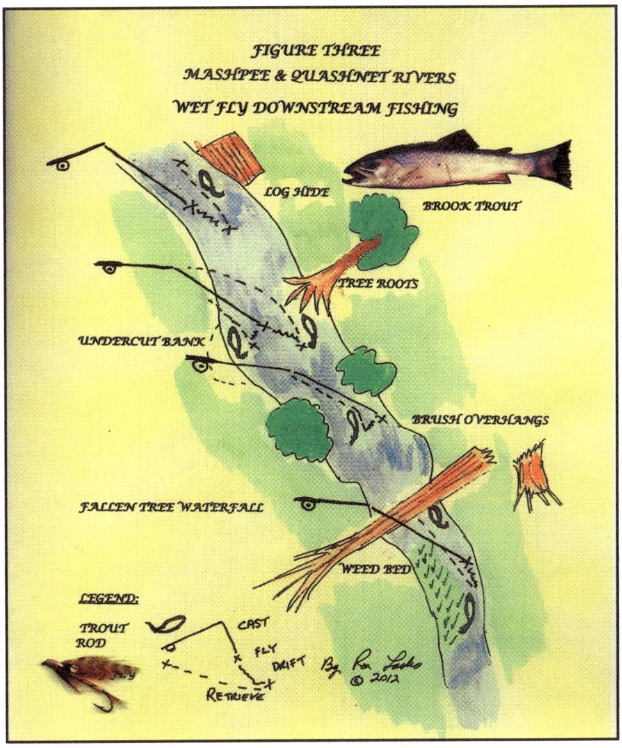

DOWNSTREAM WET FLY STREAMER

Refer to Figure Three

The Simple Drift Cast (or Non-Cast)

This is really a non-cast. No casting is ever necessary in downstream wet fly-fishing. But there is a need to codify. Merely let the current take your fly, leader, and line downstream as you strip line from the reel and feed the line through the rod guides. Try and maintain some tension as a trout may take this fly as it drifts downstream.

The Overhead Cast

When room is available for a back cast, the standard overhead cast is used followed by the simple drift. Most of the time there will be little room for a back cast when fishing downstream in these rivers, due to foliage obstructions. This cast can be made across your opposite shoulder (crossover cast) to avoid foliage.

The Sidearm Cast

This is the Overhead Cast being made horizontally, usually waist high, on either side of your body to avoid obstructions.

The Wave Cast

This is simply waving your rod with a short length of line in the air enough to get some line and leader on the water, in order to make the Simple Drift. This works well in these tight quarters.

The Roll Cast

This is accomplished by raising your rod and arm, thereby pulling the line drifting in the current before you. In one steady sweeping pull and downward thrust, you will be able to roll out some of the flyline, which will carry the leader and fly outward and land it for another drift. This can be done to the right or left side, and occurs in full frontal view of the angler so one may avoid the foliage.

Mending Your Line Right or Left

As your line is drifting, regardless of what cast you used, you can move the line, leader, and fly by pointing your rod to the right or left and moving some additional line in the same direction as you strip it off the reel. This allows you to drift your fly more to the right or left side of the stream. You will want some drifts in the center of the stream, while others may be nearer the right or left bank depending on the location of trout hides. In Figure Two, trout hides are found intermittently scattered on the right and left sides along with some trout holding areas in the center of the stream.

Simple Wet Fly Swing

Swinging your fly across and in front of a trout is accomplished by merely stopping the drift. The current will swing the fly for you as if it were a pendulum. You may extend the swing by following the swinging fly with your rod in the direction the current is taking it. This is the centuries-old classic, and is a successful basic method of taking trout. Baitfish, nymphs, and drowning or hatching insects all move across currents in this fashion and fly patterns manipulated in such fashion have always been successful when the trout is in the mood, the fly is right, and the fly swing is directly in the trout's line of vision. It also appeals to the trout's predatory instincts.

The Rod Hold

After the swing you may allow the fly to just hold in the current below you. The current will move the fly naturally a few inches side to side. This fly, held in the current for a length of time determined by the angler and given some slight movement by the current, may encourage a hidden trout nearby to come out.

The Rod Pull & Twitch

At the end of the drift and swing the rod may be pulled toward the angler, causing the fly to move in the direction of the pull. This movement may be a dart, a twitch, or a series of fast or slow darts and twitches, made by the angler merely moving the rod in any desired direction or angle. This alerts the trout to an insect or baitfish that is alive and in reach. These movements may be the length of the rod or just inches, depending on the angler. Since there is tension on the line, trout will often hook themselves unless the angler pulls the fly away. A white-winged wet fly or streamer will demonstrate fly movements and help the angler appropriately coordinate all wet fly and streamer retrieves and movements. Try stop and start retrieves.

The Hand Twist Retrieve

At the end of the drift, swing, and rod manipulations, the angler retrieves. This, of course, prepares for another cast or drift, but it also offers the possibility of enticing a trout to take. By moving the rod to either side during the retrieve, the fly may be brought along and through the various stream habitats to move the trout holding there. In this retrieve, the angler lightly holds the fly line with one hand against the cork grip while gathering the retrieving line in the other free hand. This retrieve can be made slow or fast, depending on the angler. This allows the fly to appear to be swimming past and away from the trout or through the trout's territory creating interest. The line held lightly against the cork with one hand maintains the tension to hook a taking trout.

The Hand Strip Retrieve

Instead of twisting the retrieving line in the free hand, the angler strips in line with the free hand letting it fall after each pull. This can be a strip of a few inches or several feet depending on the movement the angler wants to create. Again the tension for hooking a taking trout is maintained by the hand holding the line against the cork grip. The fly may be moved through the current in directions and angles determined by the angler as he moves and points the rod during the retrieve. Try zig-zag styled retrieves.

The Rod & Line Strip Retrieve

This uses the rod as well as your hands to retrieve. The rod is pulled toward the angler and then the line is stripped, or they are done in concert, or interchangeably to vary a darting, stop-and-go, fast-and-slow, or twitching movement of the fly.

Cast, Strip, Drift, Sink

This method is intended to sink the fly deeply when fishing a deep section of water. It works best on deep, slower moving water, such as the lower Quashnet. On our little rivers this works well with an intermediate line, but will also work with a floating line. Using a cast of his choice, the angler strips line and lets it drift as the fly line and leader sink deeper than the original cast. The angler then strips more and more line to continue drifting, allowing the fly, leader and line to go deeper until the depth level is achieved. Once the angler is satisfied with the depth, any of the aforementioned retrieves are used. When trout are hanging near the bottom and not moving, this method will get the fly down to them. Trout often hold deep in winter, in early spring, in bright sun, and in the heat of summer.

The Leisenring Lift

This method was perfected by James Leisenring, author of *The Art of Tying & Fishing the Wet Fly.* Following the cast, strip, drift, and sink, Leisenring would slowly raise his rod tip to make the deeply sunken fly rise up in front of the trout's nose, as if it were a hatching insect. This is a highly effective method when one is aware of a deep holding trout's location and places the fly directly in front of the trout.

The Pulling Off Technique

This wet fly method was noted by Vince Marinaro, author of *In the Ring of the Rise* and *A Modern Dry Fly Code*. Once a feeding trout is located, the angler drifts the wet fly parallel to the trout on one side or the other, several feet away, and several feet behind the trout. Then on the retrieve the fly is first brought directly across from the trout and then stripped right across the trout's nose. This is another effective method on a trout you have located that is feeding below the surface on hatching insects or drifting baitfish, and refuses to move far from his holding area. This method has proven effective for me on hatching stoneflies and caddis and on the drifting migrations of herring fry on both rivers.

WET FLY & STREAMER FISHING IN GENERAL

I use the above mentioned methods for casting, drifting and retrieving on these rivers. Oftentimes I will use a combination of many of them on a single cast or on a simple drift cast, as I work the fly along a weed bed, a log embankment, or a deep run. Also keep in mind that, whether you are fishing a baitfish imitation streamer, a winged wet fly, a hatching caddis, a swimming nymph, or a dying drowning insect, their natural movements are what you want to match in the manipulations of your fly. When you review Figure Two, note where the trout hold and where the angler casts, drifts, and retrieves the fly. Then consider what techniques and casts you would add to this diagram. It all looks and sounds more difficult and complicated on these diagrams than it really is. But once armed with this textbook knowledge, the best thing is to practice this information on the rivers fishing to the trout. Draw up your own section of stream on site or from memory and use these techniques to map out your own plan of approach to entice the trout.

DRY FLY-FISHING UPSTREAM

All dry fly-fishing is with flies that will float on or below the surface to simulate the behavior of aquatic and terrestrial insects and the reaction of the trout feeding on these floating insects. Therefore it is necessary that your fly constantly be kept dry through either false casting to shake off moisture or, when it is impractical to false cast, by squeezing out moisture between casts using absorbent materials. On dry, sunny days, my shirtsleeve works well. Tissue paper is effective and I have an amadou suede-like leather patch on my vest. On these little rivers false casting may worry the trout and needs to be kept to a minimum.

A wide variety of new modern powders, liquids, and pastes are available to help prevent the fly absorbing moisture. I still use mucilin paste, as that is what I grew up using as a boy. It is effective and, after disappearing for many years, is now available, mainly from British fly-fishing shops or enlightened American fly shops. The amadou patch was also the favorite of fly-fishers on my boyhood Catskill Rivers. It disappeared for 30 years and then recently made its reappearance. Sometimes we find in fly-fishing, as in life, that many of the old products and methods are worth revisiting and are even superior to some of the new. "Don't throw the baby out with the bath water" is a good motto to follow.

While an argument can be made that casting is not that important when wet fly-fishing, the argument will not hold water when it comes to fishing the dry fly. One needs to be able to present the dry fly naturally to the trout without putting the trout down and that takes good, solid, basic casting ability. Conveniently, the current brings the drifting fly back to you, as opposed to wet fly-fishing, where the current carries the fly away downstream.

The Overhead Cast

This is the cast that all fly-fishing is based on. Perfect the overhead cast and all other casts will fall in line, as they are all based on its dynamics.

For many years my wife, Donna, and I were consulted to train actors, who would be portraying family roles for the Astor Beechwood Mansion in Newport, Rhode Island, as they would have been in the historical time period of 1891. Part of the training would include educating these under- and post-graduate theatre students about the traditions of fly-fishing, which played an important role with British and American upper classes in the 1890s. As part of the course I would demonstrate the various fly-fishing casts, with the students taking part in the actual casting. These young men and women, who never before held a fly rod, would perfect the overhead cast in less than five minutes.

Just think of a standing large clock. Your back cast should stop at about 2:00 o'clock and your forward cast releases at about 10:00 o'clock. All casting is based on this smooth back-and-forth action of the line, with the final forward cast only as good as the back cast. With a little effort you can achieve this on your front lawn in a few minutes. With a little practice, it will be as natural as riding a bike. Once you learn this cast (and you do not need to be perfect) you will present your dry fly naturally to the trout and begin catching trout on dry flies.

The False Cast

This is actually the basic overhead cast repeated again and again without letting the fly touch the surface of the river. It is meant to dry moisture from the fly before the final cast which drops the fly onto the surface. It is also useful at measuring the length of line the caster needs off the reel to reach a feeding trout or lie. A false cast can be used to speed up the line by pulling on excess line with the free hand, speeding its movement back and forth through the guides in order to "shoot" the final cast further than one is capable of casting with the final thrust, to meet a far-off trout or holding area.

The Crossover Cast

The overhead cast is angled across your opposite shoulder to avoid foliage behind your normal casting shoulder. Think of a tilted large clock and keep your back cast and forward cast between 10 and 2 and you will do fine.

The Sidearm Cast

Move the forward and back cast on a horizontal plane between your shoulder and knee, but usually waist high, in order to avoid foliage. Imagine a clock flat on the ground and casting between 10 and 2.

The Roll Cast

This method was explained in the wet fly casting section of this chapter. It is a necessary cast for upstream dry fly-fishing on these rivers due to obstructions. Just keep aware that your fly will pick up moisture easily and you need to keep drying and dressing it between casts. I like to use heavily hackled buoyant type patterns when doing a large amount of roll casting. The most professional and best example of the roll cast may be seen in the movie *A River Runs Through It,* when Norman returns from college for his first fly-fishing outing with his brother Paul after six years. Fortunately we do not need to be that good, as our roll casts on these little rivers are generally over short distances.

The Wave Cast

This cast is also covered in the wet fly section. It is sort of a roll cast in the air and is best used when avoiding obstructions and with a breeze or wind at your back.

The Check Cast

This is the standard overhead cast, except that, as the forward cast straightens out and is ready to fall to the water, the angler pulls back on the line, allowing the fly to fall closer than the normal cast with excess leader around it. This is useful for avoiding drag, and also on the lower Quashnet for dropping your dry fly along a bank side hide without getting hung up in stream side brush.

The Curve Cast

By turning your casting hand and wrist right or left during the forward cast you will curve the leader to the right or left to avoid an obstruction or to place the fly in front of the trout avoiding the leader lining a trout.

The Bow & Arrow Cast

This is a useful cast in the heavily wooded areas of the upper Quashnet and Mashpee. The angler pulls just enough line through the rod tip (about 5 or 6 feet when using a 6-foot rod) and with the free hand grasps the line just above the leader. The rod hand holds the line tight at the cork. The line is drawn back like a bow and then released. The fly, leader, and line spring forward like a regular cast. This is an effective cast for dropping a dry fly in a tiny pocket of open water when the angler has no other way. Be careful with this cast and practice in your yard, as a misjudgment could easily end up with the fly stuck in your ear. I have suffered that indignity.

The Plop or Splat Cast

This method is the basic overhead cast, but, instead of a smooth forward finish, the angler forces the line down hard by thrusting the rod downward during the final cast. Whenever large insects like dragonflies, large, egg-laying mayflies or caddis, and grasshoppers are hitting the water with a plop or splat, this will suggest that behavior and attract the trout. This is also effective when the trout are reluctant to come out from under their hides, but know that a splat or plop means a big mouthful.

The Twitch

Use any cast of your choosing, but, as soon as the fly lands on the water, give it a small twitch by using your rod tip to lightly pull the line. It is amazing how little effort is neede for this movement. This often signals to the trout that your fly is a live insect and something good to eat. Most natural flies will twitch when they suddenly find themselves in water. Drifting, hatching insects will twitch to raise their wings and fly off. Terrestrials such as beetles, ants, and grasshoppers will do the same. Often when I am fishing upright-winged dry flies, they land askew and a little twitch not only rights the fly but often encourages a trout to take. Just be subtle, as too much of a good thing will put down the trout, although hatching skittering caddis and active grasshoppers will often allow more than one twitch per drift.

Drag

When the current between you and the fly pulls on the fly, leader, or line, it will create drag on the fly making the fly behave unnaturally. This will put off the trout. The check cast and curve cast both help overcome drag as additional line and leader will allow a longer float of the fly.

Mending Line

In wet fly-fishing, we mend the line to use drag to work the fly underwater. When dry fly-fishing we mend the line upstream against the current to prevent drag pulling on the fly on the surface. Simply roll out extra line, as in a wave cast or partial roll cast, into and against the current to slow down the current's pull on the line.

Retrieving Line

In dry fly-fishing the fly, leader, and line are all drifting toward the angler, while they drift away from him in wet fly-fishing. The angler retrieves line as it drifts back by lightly holding the line against the cork grip and stripping in with the free hand. If the angler strips too fast the fly will move unnaturally. Too slow and drag will pull the fly. So the angler needs to strip in just enough line to prevent drag, yet be able to raise the rod tip and hook a trout rising to the fly. While the wet fly angler will find trout hooking themselves, the dry fly angler must perform the hooking of the trout. If too much line is out, there may be no drag, but when the trout takes the fly, the angler may not be able to pull in enough loose line quickly enough to engage and hook the trout, thereby getting many rises to the fly, but not hooking trout. It requires a fine balance and constant attention by the angler to avoid drag, retrieve line, and yet have just enough line that will allow the hooking of the trout.

DRY FLY-FISHING IN GENERAL

Most of the Mashpee River is a typical woodland stream flowing through a forest. The upper half of the Quashnet is similar. Dry fly tactics will be similar for these areas of both rivers. However the lower half of the Quashnet is similar to an American limestone spring creek or an English chalk stream. This is smooth, slow moving, clear water filled with weed beds. The placid surface telegraphs any unnatural behavior of your fly to the trout, magnifies the abnormal presence of leader and line, and signals frightening movements such as the waving of a fly rod. The ripples created by a wading angler threaten trout , as do the movements of a particularly brightly clad angler. These conditions make successful dry fly-fishing more of a challenge on the lower Quashnet than it is in the wooded sections of the Quashnet or Mashpee. Use all the suggestions throughout this book regarding the approach, clothing, gear, rod, reel, and tackle in order to enjoy and succeed when dry fly-fishing this spring creek-like section.

TACTICS CONCLUDED

These are two lovely little wild brook trout rivers with most of the Quashnet a spring-like creek while most of the Mashpee is a forested woodland river. Use both types of fly-fishing, dry fly and wet fly on both for your optimum fly-fishing experience.

Chapter Fifteen

HATCHES & TRADITIONAL PATTERNS

THE MASHPEE RIVER HATCHES

The Mashpee River, the river most productive of aquatic insect species on Cape Cod, hosts a full range of mayflies, caddisflies, stoneflies, midges, other aquatic flies and terrestrials with a few exceptions.

Mayflies

The mayfly season begins on the Mashpee in late March with the hatching of the species commonly known as the early brown or early black quill mayfly, though it is actually dark maroon in color. This is followed by the normal mayfly hatching cycle and includes quill Gordons and early blue quills in April; Hendricksons in April and early May; March browns and grey foxes into early June; and light cahills from June through August. Summer also brings on the hatching of the large summer yellow drakes. A unique species I find hatching here in late summer is the *euphoron* mayfly, known as the white mayfly. The speckle wing mayfly from the *callibaetis* family hatches in the fall.

Along the Quashnet, this 50′ log embankment, 4′ deep hide, holds a half dozen trout. Installed 40 years ago by TU volunteers, good hatches of stoneflies, caddisflies, blue quills, blue-winged olives, and speckle-winged quill mayflies occur here.

Various species of blue-winged olives and little blue quills can be found hatching nearly anytime from April to November. Mayflies that I have not found hatching here, but which may exist in parts of the little river's micro habitats, are the *isonychia* species dun variants, green drakes, and tiny white-winged blacks (*tricorythodes* species). Though I have yet to see these last three species, I suspect they are here.

Caddisflies

The full range of caddisfly species will be found on this river ranging from green, brown, gray, amber, tan, orange, and red bodied, with mottled wings, in sizes from #16 to the large #10 red and brown caddis of late Fall. These caddis hatches can be extensive and are ongoing throughout the season on the Mashpee.

Stoneflies

All the small to medium stoneflies hatch here, including the usual cycle of the seasons with the February and March hatching of the winter tiny blacks; the springtime little black, early brown, and little reds; the late spring and summer little brown, little amber, little yellow and little green; and the autumn dark little needle stone and dark little browns. The only large stonefly I have found hatching here is the large black stonefly of March and April. The stream bottom habitat of pea gravel most likely does not favor the giant and large yellow, brown, and golden stoneflies found on most New England boulder-strewn trout streams and rivers. Some of these smaller stonefly hatches can be large in numbers and duration; I have experienced such hatches here in spring, summer, and fall.

Midges and other Aquatics

Midges are hatching all year, sometimes in massive numbers, ranging in sizes from little #24 to large #12. The color range, although predominantly black or olive, may be white, cream, tan, amber, yellow, or maroon. This river also carries a good nymph population of the swimming damselflies and dragonflies and the adults can be seen constantly on the river from late May to November.

Terrestrials

Due to the heavy forested canopy over this river ants, including winged ants, sized #18 to #10 and colored black, red, and cinnamon, can be found falling into the river on warm days as early as March and as late as December although their prime season is May to October. Sometimes, on a warm, sunny, breezy day, there are so many large black ants falling into the river that it sounds like raindrops. Inchworms are common from April to September. Black and brown beetles are a constant from April to November, with grasshoppers and crickets from late summer to fall.

Baitfish

Herring fry are available in large numbers as they migrate down from Mashpee-Wakeby Lake commencing in June and running through December.

Elvers make their appearance in February, along with the newly hatched brook trout fry. There are resident silver and golden shiners, sculpins, sticklebacks, and dace available all year.

QUASHNET RIVER HATCHES

Although the Quashnet River does not have the full complement of mayflies that are found on the Mashpee, the Quashnet does have the full seasonal cycle of hatching caddisflies, little stoneflies, and the other aquatics.

Mayflies

I have found a broad range of Blue-winged Olives (both dark olive and pale olive species) hatching on the Quashnet, from #20 to #14, occurring from April through November; they are the most prolific mayflies that hatch on this river. There are also good hatches of #16 early blue quills (actually their body color is mahogany) in April and May, #16 and #18 blue duns and blue quills from June to September, and speckle-winged quills (*callibaetis*) sized #14 and #16 hatching in September and October. These small mayflies have, at times, provided incredible sport for me while fishing dry flies on the lower Quashnet River. In recent years I have found a few early brown quills, some Hendricksons, and a few grey foxes hatching on the upper woodland sections of the Quashnet in May, as well as a few large yellow summer drakes in June. None of these were hatches of any great number or even fishable, but just the fact that these mayflies are making an appearance is a hopeful sign that the restoration to woodlands from former cranberry bogs of the upper river over the last 40 years by TU is paying off, and these and other past species will proliferate in the future.

Caddisflies

All caddisflies found in the Mashpee are found on the Quashnet from the little black caddis of early spring to the Large Red caddis of late autumn.

Stoneflies

All of the little stoneflies found on the Mashpee will be found on the Quashnet and at times in astonishing numbers in both the woodland and spring creek sections. As with the Mashpee, the only large stonefly I have found on the Quashnet has been the large black stonefly of March and April.

Midges and Other Aquatics

All Midges found on the Mashpee will be found in the Quashnet along with heavy populations of damsel and dragonflies. There are continuous summer hatches of true two-wing black gnat flies particularly on the lower spring creek section.

Terrestrials

As with the Mashpee, ants are available from April to November. The winged ants, however, have very impressive hatches from June through October on the lower river that are not found as heavily on the Mashpee and provide wonderful dry fly-fishing. Beetles are on the water in great numbers from May to October. Compared to the forested Mashpee, grasshoppers are more prevalent on the brushy, grassy banks of the lower Quashnet. Inchworms and crickets are available to the trout in the wooded upper sections.

Baitfish

Trout fry, elvers, herring fry (migrating to sea from Johns Pond), and resident baitfish species are available just the same as the Mashpee River.

SUCCESSFUL TRADITIONAL PATTERNS

Although these are wild brook trout and, at times, some of them seem to be ready to take any fly, don't count on it. These trout are as picky as any wild brown trout if there are enough of a certain species of fly or baitfish present for them to focus on. This is particularly true when dry fly-fishing on the lower spring-like creek section of the Quashnet and even the forested, more open lower reaches of the Mashpee. One may enjoy a level of success by restricting one's fly-fishing to a limited number of fly patterns. However, the fully prepared fly-fisher, intent on fly-fishing successfully year-round on both rivers, should carry a wide range of wet flies, dry flies, and streamers.

Traditional Wet Fly Patterns

The traditional down-winged or rolled-winged patterns suggested are generally available from tackle dealers with all of the following proving effective: the Coachman, Royal Coachman, Lead-winged Coachman, Black Gnat, Red Quill, Light & Dark Hendrickson, Hare's Ear, March Brown, Light Cahill, Blue Dun, Teal Blue & Silver, Grizzly King, Olive Dun, and Blue Quill. These will suggest and match mayflies, caddis, stoneflies, midges, and other insects in their nymphal, hatching adult, egg laying spinner, or drowned stages. You will want these in sizes generally from #12 through #16.

Coachman

Royal Coachman

Lead-winged Coachman

Black Gnat

Red Quill

Light Hendrickson

Dark Hendrickson

March Brown

Hare's Ear

Light Cahill

Dark Cahill

ue Dun

Teal Blue & Silver

Grizzly King

Traditional Dry Fly Patterns

The traditional up wing dry fly patterns that have proven to be successful and are also available from fly-fishing shops are: the Adams, Royal Coachman, Black Gnat, Red Quill, Hendrickson, March Brown, Light Cahill, Blue Quill, Quill Gordon, Pale Sulphur, Hare's Ear, and Blue Dun in a range of sizes from #18 to #10 depending on the species hatching. These patterns will match most anything hatching, be they mayfly, caddis, stonefly, midge, or other aquatic.

At times, it will pay for one to carry more specific down wing dry floating patterns for matching caddis and stonefly hatches sized #12 to #16, with deer hair wings from dark dun to light tan, and with bodies colored black, gray, tan, brown, amber, olive, and mahogany. A wide variety of such patterns are also normally available.

The angler will need a variety of Floating Ant, Cricket, Inchworm, Grasshopper, and Beetle patterns to meet the terrestrial dry fly challenges of summer and fall.

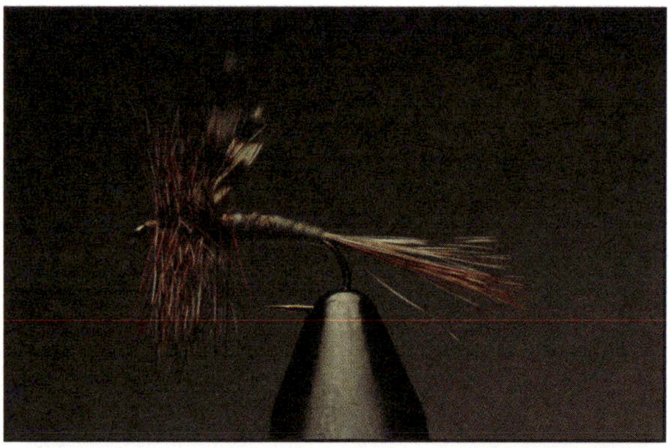

Adams

Royal Coachman

Black Gnat

Red Quill

Hendrickson

March Brown

Light Cahill

Blue Quill

Quill Gordon

Pale Sulphur

Mahogany Dun

Floating Ant

Cricket

Inchworm

Grasshopper

Streamers & Bucktails

Recommended baitfish patterns are the Silver Darter, Golden Darter, Hornberg, Gray Ghost, Grizzly King, Black-Nosed Dace and Muddler Minnow, suggestive of actual baitfish that occupy the river. The angler will also find useful traditional attracter patterns such as the Mickey Finn, Chief Needahbah, and Royal Coachman Bucktail that will move trout when other patterns fail. These bright patterns also suggest the bright colors of spawning adult baitfish. Smaller patterns are best, such as #12 and #14 in 4X or 6X long hook shanks.

Nymphs

The angler should carry a range of simple fur nymphs in black, brown, tan, mahogany, and olive colors in a variety of lengths and sizes to suggest the insects and hatches covered. The best, all-around traditional nymph to carry is the English Pheasant Tail Nymph, which has become readily available in American fly shops in recent years. Sizes carried should be from #10 to #18 in both regular and long shanks.

Golden Darter

Hornberg Streamer

Gray Ghost Streamer

Black Ghost Streamer

Grizzly King Streamer

Black-Nosed Dace

Muddler Minnow

Royal Coachman Bucktail

Chief Needahbah

Mickey Finn

FINAL NOTE ON HATCHES & PATTERNS

After 25 years fishing these rivers I continue to find new insect hatches of which I was previously unaware. I have no doubt that new hatches will continue to be found on the Quashnet in the future as the positive effects from the 50-year stream restoration projects continue to improve the habitat.

Although these traditional patterns form the basis for the angler's success, in the next chapter we will review my own favorite, very special fly patterns for fishing these rivers, which have proven to be successful over many years.

Chapter Sixteen

FAVORITE PATTERNS

The following is a list of my own favorite, very special fly patterns, which have proven at least as successful or more successful than the traditional wet fly, dry fly, and streamer patterns outlined in the previous chapter. To trumpet one's own favorite patterns to the fly-fishing community requires belief, trust, courage, and yet fear: belief that you speak from experience and knowledge; trust that fellow anglers will absorb and try your patterns; courage that you will be able to weather an attack on your ideas and concepts; and fear that fellow anglers will be either too successful using your patterns or that they will fail and blame you for it. One could simply remain smug and take no risk by just keeping what one has learned to oneself. Or one can choose to share the knowledge and experience one has gained with others, in the belief that one's concepts will be appreciated by most, and remain confident in the conviction that there is nothing to fear from a fellow angler's victory or defeat. This is the course I have chosen.

BLACK GNAT (James Leisenring) wet fly

Hook: heavy and light wire; #10 to #20
Silk: claret
Body: black secondary wing fibers from crow, wild turkey, or ruffed grouse
Tinsel: fine gold wire
Hackle: black iridescent starling body hackle or black hen hackle

Black Gnat (James Leisenring) wet fly

Full credit is given to Jim Leisenring, author of *The Art of Tying & Fishing the Wet Fly* published in 1941, for this highly successful pattern that suggests hatching black midges, black stoneflies, black beetles, black ants, tiny Winged Black Mayflies, and black caddis. This simple pattern has proved its effectiveness in the Adirondacks and the Catskills, the Battenkill in New York and Vermont, across New England, south through New Jersey and Pennsylvania, and the Great Smoky Mountains, as well as on the Mashpee and Quashnet. A major key to the success of this simple pattern is to be sure that the black body fibers and the black hackle have an iridescent sheen in them.

Avoid using dull black fibers. It is the sheen that we find in the natural insect and suggesting it within this fly helps to make the fly look alive. The thread and body fibers are twisted together into a fine rope before being wound onto the body of the hook shank.

LARGE BLACK EGG SAC (Ron Lasko) wet fly

Hook: heavy wire; #8 to #10; regular and 1X to 3X long
Silk: black
Egg sac: bright yellow fur, chenille, or florescent yellow floss
Body: black chenille, black floss or black fur
Wings: black duck secondary wing slips or dun hackle tips, splayed
Hackle: black hen soft hackle tied collar style

This egg sac pattern has proven itself when tied in a variety of hook sizes and hook shank lengths, based on matching hatches of midges, caddisfly, and stoneflies. In large 3X long sizes, #10 hooks, it has proven itself a consistent fish taker in March and April when the large black stoneflies splat down onto the surface in an attempt to jettison their eggs, enticing the picky brown trout of the Battenkill, the Catskills, the rivers of New England, and, of course, the Quashnet and the Mashpee. This is another pattern, like most of these special patterns, that requires you to or a professional to tie them.

Large Black Egg Sac (Ron Lasko) wet fly

ROYAL COACHMAN wet fly

Hook: #10 to #14 wet fly
Silk: black
Tail: barred golden pheasant tippets
Egg sac: peacock herl
Waist: red floss
Thorax: peacock herl
Hackle: reddish brown soft cock hackle
Wing: white duck quill fibres

Having read the contents of this book, you already know how I feel about the effectiveness of this classic wet fly apparently invented by a coachman in England in the 18th Century. This fly should be to the wet fly-fisher what the Adams is to the dry fly-fisher—incredibly indispensable. And yet it is virtually missing from the counters of most fly tackle shops. Several years ago I made a trip to Roscoe, New York (the birthplace of trout fly-fishing in America), in the Catskills and visited every fly shop. No one had any wet Royal Coachmans, but only the dry fly version. I finally found one small shop that had some in storage in the back room. They had about two dozen and I purchased them all. This is another pattern that you may have to tie yourself.

Royal Coachman wet fly

RUFFED GROUSE & HERL (Ron Lasko) aka LASKO KILLER FLY wet soft hackle

Hook: #12-#16 light or heavy wire
Silk: orange
Tinsel: flat fine gold
Body: bronzed peacock herl wound around orange tying silk
Hackle: ruffed grouse speckled back feather with black center

This fly is based on James Leisenring's fine pattern the red hackle. However, I find that the orange silk and ruffed grouse hackle create a more useful fly throughout the entire season, whenever similar colored caddis, stone, beetles, or mahogany mayflies are hatching or on the water. This fly has been so successful on the Battenkill, Esopus, Farmington, and Westfield Rivers that friends have started to call it the "Lasko Killer Fly." This pattern fishes best by casting across stream, letting the fly swing gently into feeding trout. This activates the hackles, simulating a struggling hatching or drowning insect. These black center, speckled hackles from the back of a ruffed grouse are one of the most successful soft hackles I have used in tying and fishing. Once the hackle is wound the outer fibers are speckled reddish brown and the black center suggests the natural darker wing case or thorax of the insect. Due to the varied color phases of ruffed grouse, some of the speckled fibers may be gray, brown, or red, increasing the shades that you may tie up to suggest other colored insects.

Ruffed Grouse & Herl (Ron Lasko) aka Lasko Killer Fly wet soft hackle

LASKO PHEASANT TAIL (Ron Lasko)

Hook: light or heavy wire, regular or long shank #10 to #18
Silk: yellow, amber, tan, orange, claret, brown, olive, black
Tail: red pheasant cock; dyed black or olive; short & long; omitted for caddis
Rib: fine gold wire
Body: 3 to 5 tail fibers wound into a rope around tying silk
Thorax: fur spun on tying silk in tan, brown, blue dun, mahogany, & olive
Hackle: partridge, ruffed grouse, hen blue dun, one or two turns. Short for nymphs & longer for hatching nymphs

The Pheasant Tail nymph has been championed by Frank Sawyer and Oliver Kite in England during the mid-20th century. George Skues, considered to be the father of nymph and wet fly-fishing in England, used these pheasant tail fibers in his patterns in the late 19th and early 20th centuries. Sawyer and Kite adapted their patterns from Skues' early works. In the first third of the 20th century, Pennsylvania's Jim Leisenring adopted Skues' use and methods into several of his own original patterns. Sylvester Nemes has also adapted these fibers into patterns in the last third of the 20th century in his trio of fine books on tying and fishing the soft hackled wet fly. I believe that the fine fuzziness that can be seen against the light when these iridescent fibers are wound around the hook shank suggests the appearance of what a trout sees in an actual insect and is what makes the pattern so successful. The standard pheasant tail nymph is available in fly shops everywhere today and enjoys a fine reputation as a trout taker all over the world, thanks to these fly-fishing authors.

Lasko Pheasant Tail (Ron Lasko)

My adaptation allows the matching of any mayfly, stonefly, or caddis, utilizing the pheasant tail fibers as the base by altering the color of the tying silk, fur thorax, and the soft hackle. By tying a thin body and thorax with a short, soft hackle on a light wire hook, one has a nymph pattern that can be cast upstream, drifting just under the surface film, fishing to trout taking shallow drifting nymphs.

Tying a fatter body and thorax with longer hackles on a heavy wire hook fishes well casting downstream in fast currents or heavy water, when hatches are about to take place and trout are actively feeding on the drifting nymphs below the surface, which are struggling to hatch.

Utilize the tying procedures outlined by Jim Leisenring in his book and by his protégé Pete Hidy in *The Book of Wet Fly-fishing*. Every created pattern is tied in the same exact method and the only differences are the color choices of silk, fur, and hackle, the size of the hook, and length of the hackle. For example, by using claret silk and mahogany fur on a #12 1X long shank hook with a dark partridge hackle you have created the imitation for a dark Hendrickson. The same materials tied slim on a 2X long hook suggest an isonychia or dun variant nymph. Using the same materials on a regular #16 hook suggests a mahogany dun (early blue quill) nymph. By using amber or orange silk and dark tan fur thorax, lengthening the tails, and winding a long partridge or ruffed grouse hackle, you have created a March Brown nymph.

The age-old advice by so many famous fly-fishers and tiers holds true today: match your patterns to the rivers and streams you fish and to the insects you find there. This is one of the most versatile nymph patterns and by using it you can match any insect and fly hatch anywhere.

Incidentally, the ruffed grouse back hackles are indispensable in these patterns. This black-centered, speckle-tipped hackle, when wound, creates the illusion of a nymph whose dark thorax and wing cases are swelling open to hatch while its speckled legs are kicking and moving. Millions of ruffed grouse are harvested every year by hunters, and these feathers are discarded and wasted. Seek out bird hunters who hunt ruffed grouse to save you these feathers or even the whole bird skin. The secondary wing quills are useful for mottled wet fly wings; the black iridescent ruff feathers for bodies and tails; the tail feathers for tail fibers or wings; the flank feathers for streamer shoulders; and the down fibers for woolly buggers and streamers. Many of the back feathers have cream to white "eyes" that can be used as a substitute for jungle cock. By utilizing more of these feathers we will better honor this prized game bird.

LITTLE BLACK GHOST STREAMER (Ron Lasko)

Hook: #12 dry fly light wire salmon
Silk: black
Tail: golden pheasant crest
Ribbing: round silver tinsel
Body: black floss
Wing: white hackle tips tied splayed
Eyes: jungle cock
Hackle: bright yellow tied sparse collar style

This is another adaptation of mine based both on the original Black Ghost streamer developed in Maine in the early 20th century and a small salmon wet fly named "The Ghost" originated on the Miramichi River in New Brunswick. I find this pattern most effective in winter and early spring, when the elvers enter the Quashnet and Mashpee after their migration following their birth in the Sargasso Sea. I believe the success and popularity of the standard Black Ghost streamer fly in New England over the last century is due to the elvers entering our rivers. When these eel fry enter in February they are transparent and the major food that is available to them are tiny black midge larvae. As they feed on these little black midges their core turns black, but their outer skin remains shiny. The tinsel roping over black floss, the glistening yellow flash of pheasant crest, and yellow hackle in our Little Black Ghost suggest elvers to our trout, which is a major food source for them until the heavy insect hatches of spring appear. This smaller, more delicate, yet active hackled, fluttering, splayed wing pattern has been more successful for me than the standard Black Ghost on these little rivers.

Little Black Ghost Streamer (Ron Lasko)

BROOK TROUT FRY (Ron Lasko)

Hook: #12 salmon dry fly light wire
Tail: soft red hackle fibers
Silk: light olive
Body: bright, light olive green floss
Ribbing: gold round tinsel
Throat: soft red hackle fibers
Wing: dyed, light, olive green grizzly hackle tips splayed
Eyes: jungle cock
Hackle: soft grizzly hackle or soft red hackle tied sparse collar style

This pattern has evolved from the standard Grizzly King streamer and from Lew Oatman's beautiful Little Brook Trout Streamer, along with my own observations streamside on the Mashpee and Quashnet of brook trout fry. In both rivers, brook trout fry are available to adult trout by the thousands from late December to April; they are a major food source, along with elvers, before the heavy insect hatches later in the spring. Brook trout fry are often brightly colored. I wanted a small lively pattern more suitable to these little rivers. This small pattern captures the bright red, gold and green coloration of the fry along with their distinctive parr markings. The splayed, working wings and the moving fibers of the collar-wound hackle give a good impression of a live trout fry as the fly is worked gently in the current.

Brook Trout Fry (Ron Lasko)

THE FLUORESCENT SPRUCE (Ron Lasko)

Hook: #12 salmon dry fly light wire
Silk: florescent red nylon
Tail: 2 or 3 peacock sword tips
Rear body: florescent red nylon lacquered multiple times
Front body: bright green peacock herl
Wing: silver badger tied splayed
Hackle: silver badger tied collar style

I clearly adopted this pattern from the standard Light Spruce streamer, along with using the florescent nylon of salmon patterns. I wanted a body that would hold up, as the floss body always shredded after a few trout. I also sought a body that was brighter, so the lacquering of the red florescent nylon not only makes a body that looks alive while standing up to trout's teeth; the red finish of the head adds that extra bit of color. It takes about five thin coats of lacquer to get the body just right. It will seem to glow. This is another splayed wing and collar hackled pattern that looks and acts alive in the current, and the peacock sword tail fibers move like a baitfish trying to get away. When trout are looking for a bright fly this is one of my favorite patterns. It is also extremely useful for moving trout when they don't seem to be interested in other flies. This pattern suggests any of a number of spawning male baitfish in these rivers, whose sides range from bright orange to red along with dace-like stripes. The silver badger dark stripe hackle is also suggestive of elvers. I also tie the same pattern using maroon nylon in place of the florescent red which develops a more subtly colored pattern which I prefer on bright sunny days over the Florescent Spruce. I simply call it the Maroon Spruce.

The Fluorescent Spruce (Ron Lasko)

LASKO SILVER BLUE SPRUCE (Ron Lasko)

Hook: #12 salmon dry fly light wire
Silk: black
Tail: peacock sword
Body: rear half-silver tinsel
Body: front half—greenish peacock herl
Wing: silver badger splayed
Eyes: jungle cock
Hackle: bright, light blue, wound-collar style

This pattern has been modeled after the English sea trout pattern known as the Teal, Blue and Silver. I find that in the fall herring fry have a bright, light blue sheen or cast to their overall silver coloration, while they seem to lack this color in the late Spring or Summer, when they appear more silvery. By incorporating these colors in the spruce streamer-style of tying, I have the movement of the wings, collar, and tails along with the late season coloring of these fry. Although the herring fry body sides are not striped, there is a faint, narrow, dark, lateral line to them. This pattern is also suggestive of a variety of natural baitfish in the river. The aforementioned Teal, Blue and Silver English sea trout wet fly works well as an imitation of these late season herring fry and I suspect these fry may have been part of the reason for the creation of this English pattern, as so many of their Lochs are accessible by herring, trout, sea trout, and salmon. The popularity of the dry fly, light wire salmon fly hooks on many of these patterns is a result of good balance, good hooking qualities, and the perfect length in a size #12. Also, being tempered black, one may fish flies tied on these hooks in the salt or brackish estuaries of these rivers without rusting the hook.

Lasko Silver Blue Spruce
(Ron Lasko)

LASKO HERRING FRY (Ron Lasko)

Hook: #12 salmon dry fly light wire
Silk: black
Body: silver flat tinsel
Wings: narrow, soft mallard flank tied normal or splayed
Eyes: jungle cock
Hackle: soft hen grizzly, tied-collar style

I adapted this pattern from the English sea trout pattern known as the Mallard & Silver and the American Hornberg pattern (meant to be fished dry and wet). Both are useful in suggesting small baitfish, such as herring fry. However, I found no need for the under wing yellow feather in the Hornberg, nor did I find that its usual stiff, mallard flank sides and heavy hackle collar were lifelike in these little rivers. The British Mallard & Silver failed in lifelike qualities as well. These herring fry are available to our trout as they migrate down the rivers to the sea from June to December so, after much experimenting and testing, I settled on the above pattern as the most effective. The herring fry are silvery with tiny scales and the silver tinsel body, so the mallard flank feathers match this feature well. I found that the fly tier needs to choose the finest, thinnest, longish mallard flank side feathers for maximum movement. These longer, softer flank feathers have more of the spherical ovoid shape required to mimic the fry. Their movement is enhanced further by tying these wings in the splayed fashion. Avoid using the heavy, thick, stiff mallard flank feathers as they lack movement qualities that are needed in the water. The herring fry have very prominent eyes and head. By adding the jungle cock eyes with a soft hen grizzly hackle, wound collar style, I was able to achieve the shape of the herring fry head and eyes and created additional head movement at the same time. This pattern has proven very successful, imitating herring fry from June into October and is used in conjunction with the Silver Blue Spruce in fall and early winter. It is also suggestive of early season sucker fry.

Lasko Herring Fry (Ron Lasko)

G.S. CADDIS (George Schlotter) dry fly

Hook: #12-#20 dry fly light wire
Silk: amber, orange, tan
Body: tan, brown, green, gray or yellow
Hackle: one red cock, one grizzly cock (wound blended like an Adams)

When George Schlotter took over the Battenkill Anglers Nook Fly Shop on the Battenkill River at Shushan, New York in 1970, he experimented with and introduced this dry fly pattern. It is one of the easiest dry flies to tie (no wings or tail) and simply one of the deadliest for taking trout. I have grown so fond of it over the last forty years that I will not venture forth on any stream without a bunch of these in my flybox. It suggests hatching caddis, moths, stoneflies, midges, and terrestrials. Almost any full day fishing on any river will find time to utilize it. I believe the blended dry fly red and grizzly hackles allow light to play through them giving the illusion to the trout that the fly is an insect that is fluttering alive even when fishing it dead drift. I believe this is the same reason that the Adams and Art Flick's Grey Fox Variant are both successful. The trout believe these flies are alive and they take them. This pattern is a super fly when fishing to hatching caddis and a great companion to the time-honored Adams dry fly.

G.S. Caddis (George Schlotter) dry fly

G.S. BLUE QUILL (George Schlotter) dry fly

Hook: #16-#20 dry fly light wire
Silk: black or gray
Tail: blue dun
Body: wild turkey wing slip, individual fiber, scissor-trimmed lengthwise
Wings: fine duck quill wing slips or dun hackle tips
Hackle: light or dark blue dun cock

This is another pattern developed by George Schlotter of the Battenkill Anglers Nook at Shushan, New York in the 1970s. The first time I used this pattern was during a heavy hatch of blue quills at the Route 313 bridge pool. This bridge delineates the border of Vermont and New York. I was having difficulty in raising trout to take my standard, traditional striped peacock, quill-bodied, Blue Quill dry flies. About fifty trout were rising all around me. I decided to try George's pattern and began taking trout after trout. It was one of those mind blowing days and I hooked and released over two dozen brown trout ranging from 7 to 15 inches before the hatch ended. Holding George's pattern against the sky, I could see that it had a fuzziness to the body along with the usual dark and light-striped body. My standard Blue Quill was smooth-bodied against the sky light. After a decade of buying many dozens of these flies (along with many other patterns) from George and unsuccessfully attempting to match the dark and light striped fuzzy body materials, George finally relented under pressure and let me in on his secret body material.

G.S. Blue Quill (George Schlotter) dry fly

It is made up of a single-fiber slip from the wing of a wild turkey. Using very fine and very sharp scissors, George would carefully cut the fiber in half lengthwise. When wound as a body material on the small hooks, it finishes out with the black and white stripe of a peacock quill but remains finely fuzzy. This tiny, fine, fuzzy, dark and light striped, segmented body closely resembles the bodies of many of the tiny mayfly species, *baetis*, *callibaetis*, *paraleptophebia*, and others, found hatching from April to November, that we call simply blue quills. It is this lightly fuzzy striped body that makes these flies irresistible to the trout.

Dry flies tied with materials, such as bird fibers to create fine fuzzy bodies, have been touted and written about in the late 20th century by Oliver Kite's contemporaries in England and our Vincent Marinaro in his book *In the Ring of the Rise*. George Schlotter has developed one of the most effective patterns for the blue quill hatches and deserves full credit for his creation, developed decades before other, more famous anglers and authors divulged their discoveries. Sadly, the Battenkill Anglers Nook has been closed for the last decade and we will no longer enjoy the unique patterns created, tested, and proven successful by George Schlotter on the picky, wild brown trout of the Battenkill.

UPWINGED ANT (Ron Lasko) dry fly

Hook: #12 - #18 dry fly light wire, regular or 1X long, depending on size of naturals
Silk: black, brown or cinnamon
Wings: white, dry fly quality hackle tips, tied upright in center at waist
Body: black, reddish-brown, or cinnamon fur as a round knob, front and rear
Waist: tying silk, tied thin
Hackle: black, red, or ginger dry fly hackle, tied spread across waist in front and rear of wings and knobs; then cut under in inverted V fashion; trimmed above so as to not obscure wings

I find that regular wingless ant patterns and the standard, wings-folded-over-the-back-style patterns are just not as effective as this upright-winged pattern. Fully spent wing patterns are effective after a heavy hatch, whenever trout are willing to take them. In observing trout behavior during winged ant hatches, I noted the winged ants will often raise their wings, which signals to the trout that this is a live ant, so they take it more readily than other ant imitations at such times.

Upwinged Ant
(Ron Lasko) dry fly

This upright-winged pattern is also more visible to the angler than a floating wingless ant, particularly when cast any distance.

Late spring usually finds large #12 winged ants on the water and, as the season progresses through summer into autumn, the winged ants become smaller and the angler will need to reduce pattern size to #14, #16 and #18. Although one will encounter the red and cinnamon ants, the predominant ant species will be black. I have found that, when #18 winged red or cinnamon ants are present, a #18 dry Royal Coachman may be effective, probably due to its ant-like, light pattern.

The inverted, V-cut hackle allows this fly to float flush in the current, which will give a natural, subtle, lifelike movement to your fly. If your fly lands askew, a gentle twitch on your part will turn the wings upright. As Vince Marinaro suggests for fishing artificial grasshoppers in his book, *In the Ring of the Rise,* a straight cast leader with the fly landing in a "crinkle" on the current flow, with the current creating the movement, is a solid tactic in fishing this fly, as the cut hackle points in the current, with a touch of subtle drag, add movement. These subtle movements of the fly, mostly achieved by the current alone, keep the fly looking alive, making our trout interested. The upright, white wings allow the angler to see the fly and set the hook at the right moment.

This dry fly pattern has been so successful on the rivers that, from June to October, I tie on a upright-winged ant before I arrive streamside, as these are so prevalent and of high interest to the trout. Of course, if, on arrival, some other insect should be active, I will change accordingly. One last point; when you are fishing a flush Floating Ant it is difficult to discern if the drag is causing the fly to drift unnaturally. With the white, visible, upright-winged pattern the angler will more clearly detect any unnatural drift and adjust accordingly.

DANCING DAMSEL (Ron Lasko) dry fly

Hook: #12-#14 regular shank fine wire dry fly
Silk: amber
Tail: none
Body: gold flat tinsel
Wing: matched pair of long narrow 1½" – 2" wood duck flank feathers
Hackle: one brown & one grizzly mixed

Dancing Damsel (Ron Lasko) dry fly

About ten years ago, on a very pleasant, bright, sunny, breezy, clear, blue-sky, July afternoon, I was fishing dry fly upstream on the lower Quashnet River. Everything was perfect about the day except that absolutely nothing was hatching and, after two hours, I hadn't moved a single trout or seen a fish rise. About halfway to "first sluice," blue-bodied, black-winged adult damsel flies began appearing out of the bank side foliage. They mated in the air and then the females would land on a stalk of ribbon weed and proceed to lay their eggs.

Ribbon weed is a triangular, stalk-like plant that grows in water with some of the stalks upright, but with most playing out and floating on the current's surface, swaying back and forth. This is one of many prolific aquatic weeds found on the lower Quashnet. It is a tough-stalked plant and often a trout can break off a fine leader by cutting through it. I decided to observe these egg-laying damsel flies and found their routine quite interesting. The females landed on a stalk and kept going down its length, inserting eggs into the it every half-inch or so. Occasionally, the current would pull the ribbon weed under the surface with the damsel flies holding on, and then both the fly and the weed would pop up above the surface. The damsel flies seemed to have a specific area of the weed in mind as they inserted the eggs, with their favorite spots being wherever the current would intermittently pull the weed stalk and the damsel fly under water.

As I observed damselfly after damselfly laying eggs in this fashion, I was suddenly startled when a ten-inch brook trout leaped in the air and plucked one of the damselflies off the ribbon weed just as the stalk and the fly popped above the surface. Twenty feet up the river I witnessed a similar event, with an egg-laying damselfly popping above the surface and a trout leaping in the air plucking the fly off the weed stalk. That was about all the observation I could stand. I tied on the experimental pattern above, which I had intended to use for the Giant Red Caddis hatches of autumn. I then sought out the trout holding pockets and holes where ribbon weed was near or even trailing over these spots. I would cast this large yet lightweight fly into these areas and give it a twitch and a little dance particularly near or in the ribbon weed and immediately began moving and catching trout. They would leap out of the air and come down on top of the fly or slash violently as it floated in or along the ribbon weed. I moved several dozen and caught ten trout ranging from seven to eleven inches fishing in this manner with this fly.

Over the last decade this fly has served me well, but only in specific circumstances has it proven itself better than another pattern. It works best on warm, clear, sunny days in July and August, when nothing else is hatching, the trout are not rising, and the damselflies are laying eggs in the ribbon weed. In the course of a normal day, it only works as well as any other pattern or not at all. I believe this pattern shows the trout a light pattern that suggests a damsel fly, and the quick little dance or twitch near weed forces the trout to make a quick decision to take the fly, which is only an illusion of the damsel fly. When the trout have other, more easily attainable food choices, they are not interested in damselfly chasing!

A black wing green damsel fly is laying eggs in the ribbon weed fronds over a 4' depth of water. A good spot to cast the "Lasko Dancing Damsel" fly pattern to move a trout hiding under the weed.

This same pattern tied on a #14 or #16 dry fly hook with normal length wood duck flank wings works well for brown caddis hatches. I always keep several of these large Dancing Damsels in my dry fly box and they have made many summer afternoons happy ones for this author.

RED BODY, GRAY HACKLE (John J. Lasko II) dry fly

Hook: #10-#14 fine wire dry fly
Silk: black or red
Tail: grizzly hackle fibers
Body: red silk or floss
Body hackle: grizzly, sparse and smaller than head hackle, not to obscure red body
Head hackle: 2 grizzly hackles, curved sides facing each other spider style

This was my father's favorite dry fly pattern, which he fished on the Esopus River in the Catskills. Initially I tied and carried this fly to honor my dad and would use it, especially, whenever I fished his rod. This fly was readily available from fly tackle shops in the Hudson Valley and in the Catskills when I was a boy, but disappeared some forty years ago. To my delight I find that it is a successful and useful fly, certainly on the rough waters of the Esopus, but also on the Mashpee and Quashnet. I believe this pattern evolved in the Catskills from George LaBranche's works *The Dry Fly and Fast Water* and *The Salmon and the Dry Fly*. In the latter book, there is a similar pattern called the Colonel Monnell used for salmon and tied on salmon hooks, while the pattern my dad obtained from fly shops in the Catskills was clearly sized and tied for trout on trout hooks.

Red Body, Gray Hackle (John J. Lasko II) dry fly

I like to use this pattern by applying a little trout psychology. When trout are feeding on sparse hatches of tiny insects, sized #24 and smaller, there are often water striders nearby attempting to intercept the tiny insect before it reaches the trout's feeding station. Often trout get so angry at such water striders that they will attack them. By pitching a Red Body, Gray Hackle above and into the trout's feeding area I have moved and taken trout that think the fly is one of those intruding water striders. It is a good summer time trick to play on our trout.

Other benefits of this fly will be elaborated upon in the next and last special favorite pattern.

THE LASKO BUMBLE (Ron Lasko) dry fly

Hook: #10-#14 light wire dry fly, regular or long shank
Silk: amber, claret, yellow, black, orange, olive
Tail: golden pheasant tippets or hackle fibers
Body hackle: grizzly
Tinsel: fine silver or gold round tinsel
Body: spun fur or floss in mahogany, tan, brown, yellow, orange, olive or black
Hackle: brown & grizzly mixed or dark dun & grizzly mixed on black bodied flies

In the British Isles, floating, heavily body-hackled patterns called "Bumbles" are used as droppers, with a wet fly on point for fishing lochs, lakes, and reservoirs from boats, and on large, rough rivers. A single Bumble is also used on smaller rivers with a "dapping" technique on a long rod, similar to what I have described as a wave cast using my short rods. However, with long fly rods upwards of 12 feet long, such flies can be "dapped" not just on rivers but also when drift fishing from boats on still waters. Such patterns are moved on the water to excite trout during hatches of the larger caddisflies, stoneflies, and mayflies. They have been used and fished in this manner successfully throughout the British Isles for centuries. No doubt the once popular, early to mid-20th century, American Catskill Bivisible body-hackled patterns, along with the Colonel Monnell patterns and my dad's Red Body, Gray Hackle pattern, evolved from these British bumble fly patterns.

From this history of both British and American patterns, the success of my dad's Red Body, Gray Hackle, and my desire for a similar different colored fly that would be effective, my own Bumble patterns have evolved to take advantage of this

The Lasko Bumble (Ron Lasko) dry fly

successful style of fly pattern. They successfully suggest larger flies when trout are taking large insects, namely the larger caddis, mayflies, stoneflies, spiders and crane flies.

My Bumbles are tied sparser and more delicately than the British patterns and are meant only to float, while the English patterns are often allowed to sink and thus use a variety of wet fly type hackles. The body hackle, combined with the mixed head hackles, imitates the fluttering wings of these hatching flies so well that, even when fished dead drift, the current provides movement on the hackle points, creating the illusion of buzzing wings and an insect attempting to fly away, thus enticing the trout. The great English fishing writer, fly tier, and author Neil Patterson takes this theory further in his book, *Chalkstream Chronicle*, by tying patterns on purpose with different sized, mixed hackles that allow the current to move the fly on its irregular hackle points and make it appear alive without drag. These patterns, tied in colors to match the naturals, have proved themselves time and again, especially when the larger insects are hatching in midstream.

A major benefit to using this style of tie on the Mashpee and Quashnet is that the body hackle helps prevent your fly from getting caught up in the streamside foliage, as happens when fishing the more traditional dry fly patterns. In fact, you may cast your fly into the foliage, bouncing it off leaves and such, and the body hackle will often prevent the hook from catching, dropping the fly to the water while making a most attractive presentation to a waiting trout. This allows you to reach fish in foliated, overhanging pockets unreachable when using conventional patterns. These are wonderful flies that maintain their floating properties longer between drying and treating the fly, when roll casting in the wooded river sections.

This is another style of fly tying and pattern that we "modern" fly-fishers have abandoned and of which a new generation of fly-fishers coming into the sport have no knowledge. And yet, their effectiveness has been documented and proven for centuries and continues today in the British Isles on sophisticated wild brown trout.

A Final Note

Iron Blue Hackle Tip

To make traditional dry flies more representative of the actual dun-colored, winged mayflies, use dry fly-quality hackle point tips in place of the traditional duck wing quill slips and wood duck flank sections. The hackle tips hold up better and more accurately reflect the light pattern to the trout. These patterns are shown in Ernest Schwiebert's classic book *Trout*.

Armed with traditional patterns and these special, favorite wet fly, nymph, streamer, and dry flies, an angler should be ready to match a fly to any challenge above or below the surface of these waters.

PART FOUR:

THE FUTURE

Chapter Seventeen

A VISION FOR THE QUASHNET

In the late 19th and early 20th centuries, this entire river system, from Johns Pond to its estuary, had been bulldozed bare, then replanted as cranberry bogs. The bulldozers flattened the contour of the little valley hillsides, stripping them of trees. Then the bulldozers ran down the remains of the river itself, ripping out its gravel bottoms and altering the river bed flows. They dug out quilt-like rectangular ditches and trenches throughout the flattened land to facilitate the watering of the cranberry plants in the newly constructed patchwork of interconnected cranberry bogs. The ditch-like, altered river flows were then broken by the installation of a series of more than a dozen sluice dams along its entire length. Their purpose was to check the river's flow and flood the bogs above. This flooding over the bogs watered the cranberry plants, prevented them from freezing in winter, and allowed a water harvest of the berries in autumn. The river and its cool springs of life, the river bed and its mayflies, the runs of sea run brook trout and herring, were devastated. A milldam was constructed several hundred feet above the estuary. This brief footage below the mill was all that was left of a three-mile river. The river was gone.

Extensive cranberry cultivation elsewhere reduced the demand and economic value of these Quashnet Valley bogs. The Great Depression was followed by a series of hurricanes that struck Cape Cod from 1930 into the 1960s, hastening their end. Salt carried by hurricane force, wind-driven rains damaged the cranberry plants. Flood waters and a raging, mud-silted trench that was once the Quashnet River ripped through the cranberry bogs and tore many apart as it searched for its long lost river bed. When the muddy waterway receded it had silted over the bogs. Many of the sluice dams were eroded, undermined, and collapsed. Facing the marginality of the economics of the cranberry business and the costs to repair, it was decided that the bogs were to be abandoned. The remaining sluice dams fell into disrepair. Brush, small trees, and bog myrtle (destructive in its own way) began growing back over the cranberry acreage. Ocean herring and sea run brook trout, having been limited to several hundred feet of habitat, were now able to take back what was left of the waterway, for the first time in 100 years, all the way to Johns Pond.

Nature was slowly fighting back. But the trout habitat was gone. The river that was once a favorite of President Grover Cleveland and the statesman Daniel Webster was now less than a mere shadow of itself. Man's destruction was so devastating that nature would need hundreds, even thousands, of years to heal this struggling little river.

In the 1960s, Fran Smith and other Cape Cod trout fly-fishers formed the Cape Cod Chapter of Trout Unlimited with a goal to restore the Quashnet to a viable sea run brook trout river. They began massive volunteer work projects on the river that included clearing out invasive, choking plant species, constructing log crib embankments with overhead cover hides, deflector wings, and underwater log roller hides, removing blocking trees and roots, cutting back bog myrtle to create a river channel, locating and digging out springs, filling in earth lowlands, forming rock berms under and above water, importing rocks for stabilizing the stream bottom, and importing spawning gravel and strategically placing this where trout could spawn once again, hand-carried hundreds of feet with buckets. Then they planted birch, oak, maple, pine, spruce, and willow trees. This Cape Cod TU chapter pressured landowners, politicians, the state, and the federal government to acquire large portions of the valley, while resisting efforts by towns to tap into the aquifer lens areas that would reduce the flow of the hundreds of life-sustaining cold springs that enter the river. They cajoled landowners everywhere to donate cedar logs from trees that were damaged or needed to be cut down, as cedar makes the best and most long-lasting log crib hides. This work continues today, a half-century later. And still the river is nowhere near full restoration.

A new 24′ log overhead hide and embankment built by Americorps on the Quashnet in 2008, creating 4′ trout hides along its length where none existed before. Photographed in June.

A September photo of the same log hide. Trout were found here just 3 months after it was built, demonstrating the value of stream restoration. Americorps workers learn valuable trades and environmental knowledge performing this work, just as CCC workers did in the 1930s.

The restoration work saw immediate returns. Brook trout began showing up, spawning, and occupying every bit of newly created habitat. Unfortunately, Massachusetts Fish and Wildlife had concluded from their own trout survivability studies in the 1930s and 1940s that brook trout on Cape Cod were doomed to extinction. Following World War II they had begun a sea run brown trout program stocking waters that the sea run brook trout had historically inhabited, but were either totally gone or had fallen to remnant populations. The Quashnet therefore was stocked every year with sea run brown trout sized 11" to 14". This annual stocking of brown trout gave the little brook trout a very hard time by occupying the best hides and feeding areas and controlling the best spawning sites, and it hindered the full return of the brook trout. But the Quashnet was a fishable, sustainable trout river once again, yielding both brook and brown trout. With TU pressure, the river was designated as an artificial lures-only catch-and-release river.

The river that was once totally devastated by man was reborn with the help of man and nature. However the rehabilitation is only partially completed. Even sections that have undergone complete rebirth need maintenance against invasive vegetation, require repair of now aging log cribbing and log hides, necessitate removal of excessive weed growth, and need annual fallen tree removals and tree replanting; all are required just to maintain the success that has been achieved. Bog myrtle in the lower, restored sections must be constantly monitored, cut back, and removed, as it infests the river bed with its roots and tries to take over the cribbing and log hides. If left alone, the bog myrtle obliterates the river channel, damming up the flow, and turns much of the river into a swamp instead of a trout stream. This maintenance work takes up so much of the TU volunteer's time that necessary new restoration work, particularly in areas that have never been restored, remains incomplete.

The rebirth of this river was a monumental achievement. The river has made a major comeback from near death but could be too easily ruined again.

At its source, Johns Pond is now ringed with housing developments of more than 1,000 homes, all releasing their effluents via septic systems which percolate into Johns Pond and the aquifer lenses that form the springheads into the origins of the river. Underground pollution plumes of a wide variety of carcinogens and contaminants from the nearby military base have made their way to the drinking water wells around the pond and into Johns Pond itself, a trout lake in its own right.

The several hundred acres of cranberry bogs immediately below Johns Pond, owned by the town of Mashpee, from which multiple springhead flows combine with the outlet of Johns Pond to form the beginning channel of the Quashnet, are contaminated by EDB, a carcinogen from jet fuel spills that have entered the aquifer from the military base. The contaminated cranberry fruit has been banned from agricultural sale. The military has installed a water treatment plant here, at a cost to taxpayers of millions of dollars, with a probable treatment period of 30 years or more before the plume over the aquifer is completely cleaned up. But there are no engineering guarantees that this will fully work; it may require many more years or additional new systems and treatments. The construction of this plant caused further damage to the already compromised springheads that were damaged in the construction of the bogs. EDB has been found in the flesh of all aquatic and marine life in the Quashnet, including our brook trout. No doubt, like the old compound DDT used extensively in the 1950s on Cape Cod, EDB is being concentrated in the herons, osprey, kingfishers, and mergansers that prey on the brook trout. We may partially restore the physical character of the Quashnet to return the brook trout only to be met with the death of the river by chemical pollution.

These town-owned bogs have been a major source of pollution to the river since before the discovery of the chemical contamination from the military base. The Town of Mashpee leased these bogs for $100,000 annually. When they were constructed, the bogs destroyed several thousand yards of the upper river. In addition, the cranberry growing process includes spraying herbicides, insecticides, and fertilizers. These chemicals that entered the river from the bogs were polluting the entire system.

The fertilizers cause nitrogen overload, creating excessive weed growth throughout the river. This excessive weed growth is so bad that, if left unchecked in the river in summer, it will back up sections of the river into the overgrown old bogs downstream. As the water drains back into the river, it brings silt that destroys spawning gravel and aquatic larvae and eggs.

These cranberry bogs cause another problem. The practice of sanding involves spreading sand throughout the bogs to improve the mineral content of the bogs and increase the yield of the cranberry fruit. This occurred naturally where wild cranberries grew in moist areas on the lee side of beach sand dunes. This sanding practice results in rain and irrigation waters washing the fine sand particles into the river and estuary causing more siltation problems.

These bogs also draw thousands of gallons of water out of the aquifer daily to irrigate the cranberry plants. This is water that would normally seep into the Quashnet as cold spring water. Instead the flow of the river is reduced. The river's water temperature is raised and the cold springs that are the life blood of the river dry up. This irrigated water is used by the plants and cranberries or evaporates into the air. Whatever residual water makes it to the river is heated up, reaching trout killing temperatures in summer.

The lower Quashnet, whose banks were flattened and planted over into cranberry bogs. Today, bog myrtle has created good, deep trout holding cover, but requires constant cutting by TU to prevent the myrtle from crossing over and obliterating the river bed.

At the end of the town bogs the Quashnet Valley Golf course begins. Here a single channel forms the river and its banks are vegetated. Golf courses are notorious for draining the underground aquifer for irrigation of greens and fairways, causing reduced springhead flows, and for their heavy use of herbicides, pesticides, and fertilizers that all percolate or drain back into the groundwater and surface water. And the golf course has added housing developments along the river, sending more septic effluent into the underground aquifer and springheads along the river. It is common knowledge that the excess weed growth in the Quashnet intensified following the opening of the golf course in the 1980s.

Before curtailing cranberry production due to EDB, when the town cranberry bogs and the golf course were jointly pumping irrigating waters from the aquifer during the dry hot summer months of June to September, anglers would readily detect the lower river levels in the woodland section of the Quashnet caused by the reduction of the springhead flows. When they were not pumping the levels of the river would rise, only to lower again when they began pumping.

So what can be done to preserve this reborn river and ensure that the necessary additional restoration continues, and that its land, springheads, and water quality are improved and maintained, so the population of wild sea run brook trout continues to thrive?

Over the last 20 years, many good things have happened. Maintenance work and new restoration work by Trout Unlimited continues, along with some help from government work force programs. Additional land along the river corridor has been acquired, increasing the buffer zone controlled by Fish and Wildlife. An automobile graveyard along the river was removed and the land remediated. The Waquoit Bay Estuary Society has formed an Institute near the river and is active in conducting studies of the river and its estuary, where the shellfish beds are closed due to chemical contamination. NOAA and the Woods Hole Institute have taken an interest in the river and in maintaining and increasing the sea run brook trout and herring populations. Massachusetts Fish and Wildlife stopped the stocking of brown trout in 1993 and the result is more and larger wild brook trout in the river. In fact, F & W has assisted TU with stream restoration work, fish counts, and support at the local, state and national level, and has taken an ownership interest in the success of the Quashnet River Restoration Project. They have installed computer fish counters on the river activated by inserting computer chips into the trout. The cost of the equipment and additional volunteer labor has been contributed through financial and volunteer assistance by Trout Unlimited. Such scientific studies will prove whether this genetic strain of brook trout use the estuary and the river, and if some are using the sea and the lakes. If confirmed, this will put further pressure on the politicians and legislatures to pass laws to curtail the despoilers. Ironically, the contamination by the military base of the town cranberry bogs with EDB has stopped the damaging use of pesticides, fertilizers, sanding, and water extraction, as the farming of the cranberries is no longer allowed. Is it a trade of one combination of pollutants for another that is potentially more sinister? Killing trout by using ruthless development practices and sand is atrocious. But having it done by the our military with needlessly discarded chemicals, is a breach of the ultimate trust. At least the cranberry bog growers' pollution has stopped and the military pollution is being addressed.

But something good and even more powerful has occurred. The average citizen, if only one by one, is learning what has happened and what it takes to restore a devastated river. This, in my opinion, is what is needed to stand the test of time.

But some bad things have happened over the last 20 years. More of the contiguous forest land as been lost to housing, commercial, and school developments. This forest land should have been added to the river buffer zone, but now it is beyond the possibility of acquisition. The grouse, quail, and woodcock have been the immediate losers and it is possible the river will be the ultimate loser. Traditional thinking that a short buffer zone will save a trout river is myopic and needs to be expanded. The shellfish beds have been closed in the estuary. The eel grass that sustained ducks and geese is nearly gone. This same vegetation supports aquatic life and trout and without it we lose trout, herring and their food sources, in addition to waterfowl .

So where do we go from here?

I believe we need to develop an overall plan, followed by all entities, in order to continue the vital maintenance and restoration of the river. This may involve a coordinating board that will monitor all activities, with the final goal of a full restoration of the river from Johns Pond through Waquoit Bay to Nantucket Sound and the sea. Let's imagine areas that an overall plan could address to reach that ultimate goal.

First, as the origin of the Quashnet, (and the origin of its smaller historical sister, the Childs River, also in need of rehabilitation) the integrity and quality of the water in Johns Pond needs to be improved and maintained. This will require land use changes and septic controls and restrictions. It will require sacrifices made by the lakeside homeowners, and they will need to understand the long term benefits they will receive.

The Town of Mashpee-owned cranberry bogs must be removed and the land rehabilitated back to a mixed, native tree forest of cedar, hemlock, pine, oak, and maple. In conjunction with replanting the forest, an appropriate channel river bed for this important section of the Quashnet should be created. The military will need to continue to cleanse the aquifer until the job is done. The Town of Mashpee needs to be held accountable for any cleanup of residual pollution of the land and the river from these town-owned bogs.

We have a unique opportunity. In conjunction with rehabilitating these bogs, we could create areas that can be accessed by handicapped anglers and their assistants. As more of our population reaches its senior years, and veterans and others need to rebuild their bodies and spirits, we can rebuild a wild, sea run brook trout section of fishery for them. We could also make this area available to other programs such as Casting for Recovery, a program designed to introduce fly-fishing to women who have suffered from breast cancer, and rebuild both their physical and mental well being.

Residential, municipal, and commercial development needs to be curtailed. Additional buffer lands need to be acquired as soon as possible. Tapping into and extracting more and more water from the aquifer must end. The Quashnet Valley golf course needs to look at other methods of maintaining their course that eliminate chemical use and minimize water extraction. After all, the original golf courses in Scotland were meant to be played in "rough conditions," without the perfect fairways and greens that we, here in America, have created. Golf courses must not be allowed to reduce the flow of our rivers and drain chemicals into them, just because they own land contiguous to a river.

A toxic spill of chemicals or oil from an accident on either Route 151 or Route 28, both main thoroughfares for moving such goods and supplies, could wipe out the trout, herring, and aquatics of the entire river. A recovery area should now be constructed to minimize the impact of such an event. Our local, state and federal authorities and responders should be fully prepared to handle such a potentially deadly, river-destroying event.

The river from Route 151 south to the herring ladder needs to be restored, which will add an additional mile of fishable water when completed. It is overgrown and backed up into abandoned cranberry bogs. Its neglect continues to add silt deposits from Route 151 into the estuary.

A professional stream rehabilitation service should be consulted to develop a complete stream rehabilitation program and assist in short and long term plans for eliminating the sources of pollution and creating appropriate stream rehabilitation work. No doubt such recommendations will include construction needs that are beyond the physical abilities of the usual TU volunteer. Grants and other fund raising efforts will be required to achieve these construction rehabilitation goals.

The herring run ladders at Johns Pond and at the site of the old millpond should be rebuilt for both visual beauty and sound functioning. The Brewster herring run on Stony Brook has been constructed with natural beauty and stonework instead of the stark concrete laboratory structures that exist on the Quashnet and elsewhere. It seems that beauty is as endangered as our trout. We will need to re-establish the mayflies and other aquatic species that have been eliminated by past practices, utilizing biologists, scientists, and Fish and Wildlife, along with TU volunteers.

Pedestrian and angler footbridges should be installed at intervals across the river to join the banks and the trails for hiker and angler alike. Pedestrian covered bridges would be suitable here in New England and would enable an angler to enjoy a break or a lunch while looking upriver and down for rising trout regardless of weather.

The current Quashnet River fishing regulation that allows only one lure, but does not address the number of hooks on that lure needs to be changed. A catch-and-release stream is not a place where anglers should be permitted to use a single lure loaded with treble hooks. Too often I have found dead or severely injured trout along the river because the angler had a difficult time unhooking a trout from such lures. Fortunately the weed growth along the river makes use of such spinning lures nearly impossible from July to October. A single, barbless hook fly is the answer. This has been proven the world over to allow a near 100% recovery of released trout. These trout are too few and too valuable to fail to give them every opportunity. Spin fishers should learn the simple basics of fly-fishing in order to fly-fish these rivers, as is required on most catch-and-release rivers around our country and the globe. We are not trying to build an elite angler but we are trying to maintain a fishable head of unique trout. There are all prices of fly-fishing outfits available, suitable to every economic level, with many less expensive than a number of spinning outfits. And besides, fly-fishing is simply more fun.

Once we have a chemically clean river with a suitable, cold water trout habitat, running its entire length from Johns Pond to the Waquoit Bay estuary, we will have plenty of sea run brook trout.

Chapter Eighteen

A VISION FOR THE MASHPEE RIVER

As previously reported, much of the Mashpee River never had to endure the ravages that took place on the Quashnet River. Land acquisitions along its banks took place along the Mashpee long before they were under consideration on the Quashnet. The mid- to lower mileage have good deep natural pocket holes for trout habitat. The spawning gravel beds are extensive. Trout are prolific and readily found in size and quantity. The full range of mayfly hatches is readily observed. And so, little attention has been given to the condition of today's Mashpee or the threats it faces now and in the future. This little river has many problems similar to those of the Quashnet, and a few unique to its own character. Although it has better water quality, it, too, is a river in trouble.

Mashpee-Wakeby Lake is its origin and the river's problems begin here. Underground pollution plumes from the military base flow on the aquifer and are close to entering the underground springs that create this trout lake in just a matter of a few years or even months. Once in the lake, these chemicals will find their way into the Mashpee and spread contamination. As with Johns Pond, thousands of homes ring the Lake and its uplands and their septic and chemical household effluents make their way underground into the Lake and the river. After 30 years of fishing the river, I have noted that, in the past decade, aquatic weed growth has intensified and the likely culprit is nitrogen loading from residential septic systems. Water extraction, through drinking wells and for lawn sprinkling systems, reduces the springs and their crucial cold water flows into the lake and the river. The continued enlargement of residential lawn systems calls for herbicides, pesticides, and fertilizers, adding to the contamination and nitrogen loads in the lake and river.

The river begins at an innocent looking concrete dam and herring ladder at the south end of the lake, which raises the lake water level and travels south for several hundred feet to a man-made pond at the Route 130 bridge. This unnecessarily dams the river, creating a warm, shallow pond. An ugly, concrete herring run ladder system has been installed here with a pedestrian bridge and a large, adjacent macadam parking lot that drains road tar and car wastes into the river. The river then flows ditch-like through overgrown abandoned cranberry bogs, going counterclockwise for several hundred yards before crossing Great Neck Road. Just before crossing Great Neck Road, the river is joined by the outlet of a large, natural, shallow, warm-water pond. The dam at the lake outlet and the shallow pond contribute to this section of the river running at 80 degrees from July to September—a lethal temperature for trout. There is little to no structure here to hold trout or other fish. After crossing Great Neck Road, the river continues flowing south through more overgrown, abandoned cranberry bogs. It is subject to road contamination runoff, residential, commercial and municipal town buildings, and their septic and lawn contamination.

The river flows through these old bogs with little to no overhead cover and nearly no structure until it reaches the forest woodland, some 1,000 yards further south. Finally, shade and continuous running cold springs above ground and in the riverbed itself drop the water temperature to trout-supporting levels. However, more homes keep appearing along the river banks and each wants a good view of the river, so they clear cut the woods to the river bank and install green grass lawns. This is the action of landowners who should know better and be fully aware of what damage their actions are causing by eliminating streamside vegetation and tree cover, and by the nitrogen loading from their lawns. Their visionless, selfish actions reduce trout cover, warm the river, send more nitrogen and chemical contaminants into the river, and take away the vegetation needed by the hatching aquatic insects. Trout will not spawn where there is no cover. The end result: no trout here and a lot less trout for the entire river system.

The upper Mashpee River in August, showing a watercress bed on the left and blueberry bushes opposite.

Finally, the little river makes its way past these residences into several miles of fully forested, overhead canopy, with heavy streamside vegetation; the sea run brook trout appear in nearly every natural, cover habitat area. For the next several miles, to the estuary, the water rarely gets higher than 62 degrees and the trout thrive.

However, an observant person will see that our little river is not out of the woods yet. Indian Meeting House Road parallels the river in a southern direction and is separated from it by a wide swath of forest. Beginning at and opposite Asher Path (a dirt trail) is the Town of Mashpee Landfill (dump), which is sited on higher ground. Contaminants from the landfillhave been found to be flowing underground into the river for nearly half its final mile to the estuary. Also, at Asher Path the trails have become a favorite of All Terrain Vehicles (ATVs) and other on- and off-road vehicles. Such vehicles cross the river here and churn up sand and silt sediments; that siltation flows throughout the lower river, covering spawning areas and aquatic insects. Sometimes the siltation from these vehicles actually discolors the river for hundreds of yards. These vehicles access the river from recent residential developments on the opposite or west forested banks. These residences add more effluent contaminants, nitrogen, and water extraction to the list of threats diminishing the river and its trout. From the landfill to the recent residential developments, these threats have all manifested themselves in just the last 15 years.

At the estuary, the river is joined by the outlet of a small, cold water pond named Trout Pond. During the last 15 years, it has been proposed that a Performing Arts Center be built, abutting the south shoreline. While fundraising proceeded, acres of forest were cut down to accommodate its planned 500-seat theatre and a parking lot. Nearby, condominiums sprang up, abutting the line of the preserved forested river bank. Developers love to build along parks and preserved forests in spite of the pollution they cause. These areas of Trout Pond exploited by the developers have already eliminated what had been grouse, quail, and woodcock covers. Now the birds are gone and the river is threatened further.

The vestige of a c.1900 cedar log hide on the Mashpee River. Several of these remain, along with side-channel trout stews. The then private club members were college professors who probably learned these practices from their British counterparts who fished the famed English Test and Kennet.

There have only been a few good things happening to the Mashpee River over the last several decades, as most of the news has been bad. Massachusetts Fish and Wildlife did cease stocking brown trout in the river in 1993 and the sea run brook, no longer in competition with large, stocked, brown trout, have improved in quantity and size. The 500-seat Performing Arts Center group failed to raise enough money to satisfy its major, multimillion dollar donor, who withdrew his support, resulting in a fight among the non-profit groups over the funds that had been collected. For now the center will not be built, but the unnecessary damage they caused to the forest remains. The Town of Mashpee has closed off Asher's Path from access via Indian Meeting House Road, but access from the west bank residences to the river by vehicles remains. Everything else that has happened to the Mashpee River over the last 15 years has been negative.

Unfortunately, many citizens believe that, since land has been acquired along much of the river, it has been saved and that there is no need to be concerned for its future. This is myopic thinking by conservation-minded people. The river remains threatened and needs further protection and rehabilitation now to end ongoing degradation and future loss.

So what needs to be done?

As with the Quashnet River, a specific oversight board needs to be created that has the power to stop the polluters and developers of any kind regarding activities that will damage the watershed. This board will need the teeth to tackle the town, the state, the US military, and the federal government, all of whom are failing to do what is needed to maintain a healthy watershed.

The military needs to clean up the underground chemical contamination plumes before they enter Mashpee-Wakeby Lake, along with the aquifer's lens and springs that will enter the river, causing chemical contamination.

The Town of Mashpee needs to clean up chemical contamination leading from its landfill drainage to the river. Consideration should be given to ending and closing this ill-sited dump.

The town needs to control and end the recreational vehicle damage to the river and its resultant siltation contamination by disallowing access, subject to confiscation and other remedies. The noise and movement of such vehicles greatly disturbs the grouse, quail, woodcock, wild turkey, and songbirds that this watershed provides habitat for.

Buffer areas need to be created to prevent hazardous materials from entering the river in the event of road accidents at Route 130, Great Neck Road, and at Route 28, with hazardous material remediators trained in advance to respond to such events that could destroy the insects, trout, and the river.

Current residences, condominiums, and commercial activities, including Town Office and Buildings, from Mashpee-Wakeby Lake to the estuary need to be subject to strict land- and water-use controls. Future residential and commercial development in the watershed should be curtailed.

More lands need to be acquired and added to the watershed on both sides of the river, the lake, Trout Pond, and even across Indian Meetinghouse Road where many springs that feed the river originate.

The dam and fish ladder at Route 130 should be considered for future removal. The warm, small Stillwater Pond only harms the water quality.

A stream rehabilitation company should be consulted and funds created to rehabilitate the river from the Route 130 dam through the abandoned cranberry bogs, approximately one mile, until the river runs naturally along its lower mileage. Even where the river first enters, the fully wooded forest runs overhead and bank cover needs replacement due to the impact of residences that have been built on these banks.

The forested woods along Trout Pond, destroyed by the now defunct Arts Center, which should never have been allowed to even choose this site, should be rebuilt to protect the springheads and runoff.

Catch-and-release, single-hook-fly-fishing-only regulations should be instituted. This will allow the river to hold as many sea run brook trout as possible and the excess trout ,with their sea run genetics, could be used in limited transfers to restock wild trout in nearby rivers who have lost their trout, such as the Santuit, Little, Childs, Centerville, Quaker Run, and Marstons Mills Rivers. Her wild trout could also be used, in conjunction with wild trout from the Quashnet River, to restock all other former sea run brook trout rivers of Cape Cod.

The river has a full complement of mayfly hatches that also could supply transfers and restocking to the other Cape Cod rivers whose mayfly hatches have been depleted or destroyed by past pollution and development practices. This is another major reason to do all that we can to preserve this river.

The estuary sections below Trout Pond outlet need to be scoured of thousands of yards of sediment that has accumulated over many years from the upper river, abandoned cranberry bogs, and, in recent decades, from the ATVs crossing the river bed. This sediment has killed eelgrass, baitfish, and shellfish, and eliminated trout cover in the brackish water where the trout used to feed and grow before spawning in the upper freshwater river sections. This will require professional rehabilitation and the need to involve local, state, and federal agency approvals.

The Mashpee River, with its woodlands, clean water, natural river trout habitat, wild sea run trout, herring runs, full range of mayfly hatches, and a rich history that includes famous fly-fishers such as Daniel Webster and President Grover Cleveland, is the last woodland valley, fishable sea run trout river of its kind on Cape Cod.

Her preservation will provide the mayflies and the sea run brook trout to restock the dozens of destroyed rivers all around Cape Cod.

She is still in trouble and more work needs to be done. We can not afford to lose her. She must be preserved.

Chapter Nineteen

THE FUTURE OF CAPE COD SEA RUN BROOK TROUT

Maybe the title of this chapter should be, "Is there a future for sea run brook trout and their rivers on Cape Cod?" The future remains in doubt. The essential fact is that "there must be a future for sea run brook trout and their Cape Cod rivers!" Why? Because the sea run brook trout are the canaries in the mine. When one considers that 20-plus historic rivers on Cape Cod used to have sea run brook trout, the fact that there are only two remaining rivers with a viable fishable population today means that we are about to run out of live canaries.

If we restore these trout to their historic rivers of Cape Cod, that would mean we have cleaned up our air, earth, and water of their chemical contaminants that have been poisoning our drinking water over the last several centuries. It would mean that the degradation of the land of this peninsula, that began in the 1600s, has been checked and reversed, with the land restored to healthful sustainability. The greater reason that this must be achieved is the health of the people of Cape Cod. We have the highest rates of breast cancer and high rates of many other unusual cancers, and it has been suggested that the chemical contamination of our drinking water may be a primary cause. If we do not restore the environment by returning these unique trout to all Cape rivers, then we will have failed. The odorless, tasteless, colorless chemical contamination that is found in our insects, birds, fish, wildlife, shellfish, and human beings will eventually destroy our people. We will face not only the "Silent Spring" documented by Rachel Carson as the effect of DDT, but a silent summer, autumn, and winter.

The answer is simple. If we have clean air, clean soil, clean water, and a clean river habitat, we will have sea run brook trout. And we will have saved our fellow human beings in the process. We simply must do this the survival of the human race. But as simple as that sounds the remedy is incredibly complicated.

In the nearly 400 years since the arrival of the Plymouth Colonists, the environment of Cape Cod has been plundered, damaged, contaminated, and altered by the same culture of greed that has spread across America. That same culture of greed and its destructive power continues.

To have clean, cold water, we must cleanse the aquifer of the chemical pollution emanating from the military base. There are a dozen or more plumes involved, but only a few are actually in the treatment stage. Our water is being damaged by dumpsite and landfill leaching, by chemicals from commercial and residential septic systems, by lawn spraying of the same by residential and commercial properties, by recreational site pollution, and by road tar, gas and oil runoff pollution. Twenty golf courses spray herbicides, insecticides, and fertilizers that drain into the soil and accumulate in the aquifer. The cranberry industry does the same all across Cape Cod. The Cape Cod Railroad sprays herbicides to kill vegetation along the entire width and length of its tracks. And a new serious threat has emerged. The electric utility company that services most of New England, newly purchased by investors from Great Britain, will be spraying herbicides to kill vegetation in their 500-foot wide, 90-mile long power line corridor from one end of Cape Cod to the other. This is being done so they do not have to periodically cut brush. This spraying will cause more serious contamination to the water as these power lines cross both the Mashpee and the Quashnet and will impact all the historic sea run trout waters in addition to over 125 lakes and ponds and all estuaries.

Although fish passage ladders have been built around the dams on most rivers, the genetically imprinted herring and sea run brook trout have been decimated. The first book on Massachusetts fisheries was written in 1833, *A Natural History of the Fishes of Massachusetts*, by Jerome V.C. Smith, MD. A quarter of its 399 pages were dedicated to fly-fishing for sea run brook trout on Cape Cod. Dr. Smith criticized the local Cape Cod authorities for allowing the construction of a milldam on the Lower Quashnet River, stating it would destroy its sea run trout and herring fishery. He said it had been common knowledge, in 17th century England, just how devastating such dams were to anadromous fish populations of trout and herring. He also noted that Cape Cod authorities were already fully aware of the destruction of the herring and trout runs that occurred when milldams were built in the 17th century on Mill Creek in Sandwich at Shawme Pond and on the Marstons Mills River in Barnstable.

Marker for the first fulling mill in Barnstable erected on the Marstons Mills River. The dam for this mill eradicated the sea run herring and brook trout in 1689.

His comments confirm that our Cape Cod ancestors and authorities in 1833 knew about the damage they were inflicting, but were more interested in the short term wealth that would be generated. They knew they were irrevocably damaging the fishery, but they didn't care. These dams were just the beginning of scores of dams that were built across the running waters of Cape Cod in the following years.

Every Cape Cod town's historical society has photographs from 1860 to 1880. They document that Cape Cod became a barren, treeless land, where the forests had been clear cut for firewood, building materials, and the creation of cranberry bogs. The devastation seen in these photographs is shocking. It caused a reduction in springhead flows that once cooled the rivers. The river habitat structure needed to support fish life was decimated. The warmed water would no longer support cold water species, such as trout and herring. Mercifully, over the last 150 years, trees have returned, but not to the full extent that was lost. The trout have not.

The dam for the mill site on the Marstons Mills River, erected in 1689. Today, a herring ladder has been built to allow fish passage, and herring and a marginal number of sea run brook trout appear, but the trout are shadows of the runs prior to 1689.

In the 1880s, President Grover Cleveland, disappointed at the lack of trout fishing around Washington, D.C., purchased a home with extensive acreage in Bourne on Cape Cod, near his trout fly-fishing friend Joseph Jefferson, the famous actor and portrayer of Rip Van Winkle in the Broadway play of that name, which ran for decades. President Cleveland wrote *Fishing and Shooting Sketches*, which was published in 1901. Many of the essays refer to his fly-fishing on the Quashnet and Mashpee as well as other trout rivers on Cape Cod during the 1880s and 1890s. He even interviewed the Native American who had fished with Daniel Webster in the 1840s. He told President Cleveland that he often found Daniel Webster, who lived in nearby Marshfield, Massachusetts, writing his famous speeches during fishing breaks along the Mashpee River.

President Cleveland gave up on Cape Cod and its diminishing sea run brook trout fishing in 1897. He sold his "Gray Gables" estate, as most of his acreage was to be taken for the construction of the Cape Cod Canal eliminating the ocean view and serenity he so enjoyed. The completion of the Cape Cod Canal also forever destroyed two of the finest Cape Cod sea run brook trout streams. One flowed south to Nantucket Sound while the other flowed north to Cape Cod Bay. The canal eliminated the trout and herring that had two different genetic origins. One was Cape Cod Bay to the north while the other was Buzzard's Bay and Nantucket Sound to the south. Cleveland's answer to the canal's environmental destruction of Cape Cod was to sell and move to a trout-laden wilderness area of New Hampshire for his close-to-home trout fishing and to join fishing clubs in Quebec for salmon and sea run brook trout fishing.

Wealthy Americans have always been able to move away from areas when the environment became deteriorated, and the practice continues today. Most Americans cannot or do not want to move. Many accept the deteriorated living conditions, while others choose to fight to improve their environment.

A commercial wind farm, consisting of 130 towers, 450 feet tall, is nearing the start of construction on the south shore of Cape Cod. Each turbine is the equivalent of a 50-story building, and they will be scattered over 5 miles, from Hyannisport to Falmouth. They will string across the sound and be visible from the mouths of the Quashnet, Mashpee, Little, Marstons Mills, Santuit, Childs, and Coonamesset Rivers. It will be massive. It will destroy the beauty of Nantucket Sound. It will kill thousands of migrating bird and waterfowl species. Yet our state and federal governments and their environmental agencies have pushed it through. Large amounts of petroleum lubricants will be used and spillage that may foul these sea run brook trout estuaries is likely to occur.

Denmark, which has had years of experience building similar wind turbines, recently announced that all future sites will be at least 20 miles offshore, as those built on land or within 3 miles of shorelines are too destructive to the health of people and wildlife.

Our federal government says that all future, approved sites, from New Jersey to Virginia, will be 20 miles offshore, but they refuse to change their position on this Cape Cod site.

We all know that we need to develop new sources of energy. This site, in the middle of the Atlantic Flyway, is the wrong site. It is not the first time that the local, state and federal governments, along with the business development community, have made poor decisions regarding the environment of Cape Cod and its people and it most likely will not be the last time. Eighty percent of Cape Cod residents spend only 3 to 6 months per year living here and the governments have calculated how to circumvent and eliminate these residents' positions on the environment and thereby overwhelm the 20% minority who live and work on Cape Cod 12 months a year. These absentee residents need to take a new approach to counter how they are misrepresented by government and business interests on Cape Cod. Maybe when they see the immensity of this wind farm monstrosity they will realize what they have lost. Or those who can may simply sell their property and move away.

I suppose, like President Cleveland, our modern day presidents will simply take their vacations to places other than Cape Cod and certainly will have no desire to purchase property overlooking commercial wind turbines. It is unknown just how much damage to the environment this wind farm will cause, or what litigation and damage we Americans will face should the killing of Canada's and Mexico's migrating birds and waterfowl be significant. We do know that the involved governments expect to generate tax income at the expense of the environment. That is not what wind power should be all about. It should be about saving the environment. Unfortunately, the expediency of tax income and corporate profits, under the guise of job creation, wins over the environment once again. The very environment that we have trusted our governments to protect is degraded once again. The culture of greed is alive and well on Cape Cod, in Boston, and still emanating from Washington, D.C., just as it has been too often over the last 400 years.

In 1951, Massachusetts' Division of Fisheries published a report of the results of studies undertaken on Cape Cod lakes and ponds and their outlets to the sea from 1946 through 1948. There are many references made by the fishery field managers and their technicians in this report that indicated damage to fish, amphibians, and marine life.

Field managers and field technicians conducting the studies found the use of dams and sluice dams from cranberry bogs were not only prohibiting the herring and other anadromous fish from migrating to and from their spawning grounds, but were a direct cause of actual, witnessed fish kills. Furthermore, they often found dead amphibians and dead fish in the waters around cranberry bogs, following the spraying of the bogs with unknown chemicals. They also cited chemicals used in the cranberry bogs as the primary cause of deformed amphibians living in waters near cranberry bogs and suggested that the absence of fish species in certain waters adjacent to the bogs was likely due to chemical spraying.

It is interesting to note that there is no mention in the report of the type of chemicals being used or of any effort to penalize the bog owners for the fish kills and dam-blocking maneuvers. The report was not released until three years after concluding the study. This study contributed to the assessment by Fish & Wildlife that the sea run brook trout were doomed and would shortly become extinct forever from Cape Cod waters. Hence the origin of the now failed 50 year sea run brown trout stocking program, which was curtailed on the Mashpee and Quashnet Rivers in 1993.

Rachel Carson began her career as a marine biologist here on Cape Cod at the Woods Hole US Marine Biological Lab in 1929. In the 1940s, she became Editor-in-Chief for the US Bureau of Fisheries in Washington, D.C. She wrote *The Sea Around Us* in 1951, which remained on the *New York Times* best seller list for 81 weeks, winning numerous awards and being published in 32 languages. In 1955, she wrote the companion book *The Edge of the Sea*.

In the late 1950s she was contacted by Cape Cod friends. They told Rachel of the spraying of DDT on Cape Cod, and that birds and insects falling dead out of the sky following the sprayings. More stories of such events all around Massachusetts, New England, and the northeast were relayed to her. I was about 10 years old at that time and I remember DDT spraying in my Hudson River hometown in New York. We were advised by the authorities to close our windows and not to go outside our homes the night of the sprayings, which were done after dark. When we awoke the next morning there were dead birds and insects on our streets and sidewalks. The authorities advised that we were not to worry as DDT was safe to humans.

In 1958, Rachel Carson began her own studies of the spraying of DDT and its ill effects on insects and birds. Her personal investigation and studies resulted in her 1962 book *Silent Spring,* which shook the corporate board rooms of the chemical and agricultural industries as well as the federal agencies responsible for protecting the health of Americans and the environment. Rachel was vilified and violently attacked by the chemical and agricultural industries, which mounted and funded massive campaigns against her and her book, while the federal agencies stood by silently. Carson never wavered from her findings nor retreated from the fight, even though she was suffering greatly, seriously ill with cancer.

President John F. Kennedy, a lifelong resident of Cape Cod, read her book and ordered a federal investigation of pesticide policies. It was shocking for President Kennedy to discover that the federal agencies knew of the harmful effects of DDT, but had suppressed the information for decades under pressure from the chemical and agriculture industries. He ordered a re-evaluation of all federal pesticide policies. In 1963, the Kennedy administration agreed publicly with Rachel Carson's findings, resulting in a total ban of the use of DDT.

Rachel Carson succumbed to her cancer and died at the age of 57 in 1964. Her book helped to change our use of chemicals and our thinking in the way we need to treat the environment. Her words are even more valuable today and need to be resurrected as we face a Molotov cocktail of ingested chemicals being stored in our bodies. The onslaught continues and, once again, history is repeating itself as our government agencies often remain silent. Too often we all forget the history of mankind's abuse of the environment.

Every spring, when the Hendrickson and March brown mayflies are hatching on the Mashpee River, I think of this brave woman who fought the polluters to the end. These mayflies and our small sea run brook trout populations would not exist on Cape Cod today without Rachel Carson. DDT would have wiped them out. This gentle woman, who died too young, became a giant of a human being and fearlessly turned the polluters and the government upside down.

Yet today, 50 years after the banning of the use of DDT, even newborn children have traces of DDT in them, as do birds, mammals, trout, mayflies, and ourselves.

In the late 1960s, the first and only trout stream rehabilitation project on Cape Cod was begun by Fran Smith and the Cape Cod Chapter of Trout Unlimited to attempt to restore the devastated Quashnet River. Their success has been documented by Fran Smith and others in film and slides, in numerous newspaper and magazine articles, and by the regional and national headquarters of Trout Unlimited. By the 1980s, fishable populations of self-sustaining wild sea run brook trout had returned to the restored river. The work of Fran Smith and his TU volunteers formed the foundation for moving forward to restore all the damaged historic sea run brook trout Cape Cod rivers in the future.

In 1984, when I first "washed ashore" (the name given by long term generational Cape Codders to anyone not born here) and arrived on Cape Cod as a full time resident I had little hope for the future of the sea run brook trout and their rivers. Commercial, residential, and agricultural development was rampant, with little or no thought given to the destruction of the environment that was ongoing throughout the 20th century and especially since the 1950s.

Cedar logs cut by Trout Unlimited volunteers for use in the construction of log hide trout habitat and embankment stabilization on the Quashnet River.

The woodland valley of the upper Quashnet River restored by Trout Unlimited volunteers. They constructed the 80' log cribbing run from cedar logs, like those shown in the previous photo, now holds trout who rise to an angler's dry fly during hatches.

Local town governments operated in secret. Open meetings either did not take place or were often a sham. Real estate developers and polluters always had the green light to move ahead. The power plant in Sandwich was fouling the air and water of the entire Cape. The military base had polluted the sole source aquifer and the military, the state, and the federal government all denied responsibility, often hiding behind self-serving reports by the very agencies that were charged with protecting the citizens and environment. Septic systems were inadequate or failing, and some never even existed. Lands that abutted lakes, ponds, rivers, herring runs, estuaries, and the historic, extinct sea run brook trout rivers were being taken over and developed. Herring populations were disappearing. Shellfish beds were closing due to contamination. Cranberry bog spraying was unmonitored. Golf courses were going up all over, bringing their subtle pollution without any management plan. Heavy water extraction through well creation was reducing the springhead levels in rivers without any management plan. Some town water pipes were lined with asbestos. Cancer rates of many types greatly exceeded the normal levels found elsewhere in the state or in the entire US.

My employment position often required me to travel across the nation, sometimes for several weeks at a time. On my return, I was often shocked at how the landscape of Cape Cod was disappearing literally overnight while I was gone. In just a few weeks, I hardly would recognize sections of the Cape. One week there would be a forest. Three weeks later it was gone, replaced by a development of 50 homes under construction.

We were experiencing a race among developers and towns to build everything as rapidly as possible and ignore any environmental concerns, the likes of which Cape Cod had never seen. The culture of greed was eating its way through every town on Cape Cod. Quick profits for developers and the promise of hefty, immediate tax returns to the towns, the state and, the feds were all that mattered. Who would build the quickest and reap the fastest profits and taxes? It was an ugly, wild west gold rush, devastating this fragile island peninsula while state and federal agencies stood by, ignoring the permanent long-term damage being done to the environment that was going to cost us all eventually.

The local Trout Unlimited volunteers expressed dismay and despair at the attitudes of developers, the towns, the state, and the federal agencies. The fear that the small remaining populations of sea run brook trout in the Mashpee and Quashnet rivers would become extinct was real. The myopic, roughshod, and mindless development that was occurring in those years on Cape Cod, without thought, without care for the environment, and without a resource management plan, rivaled that of any development in the United States.

But a non-violent revolution was brewing. Citizens began standing up one by one, expressing their resistance to what was taking place. They got knocked down. Then they would increase their numbers and get thrown back again. Then they would add their own experts to enter the fray and slowly, oh, so slowly they began to slow the tide, however slightly. Citizens finally began to realize that the governments and their agencies would do little to help. Citizen groups knew they were doing the right thing and they forged ahead and began to earn first small, then larger victories.

In 1981, Citizens for the Protection of Waquoit Bay was formed and, in conjunction with other organizations, was successful in having the state create the 2,800 acre Waquoit Bay Reserve, which included the Quashnet River Valley. In 1987, the Federal Environmental Protection Agency (EPA) authorized the National Oceanic and Atmospheric Administration to create and establish National Estuarine Reserves. By 1990, the Waquoit Bay Reserve became a joint state and federal reserve now known as the Waquoit Bay National Estuarine Reserve. Their goals, among many others, are to restore the habitat, fish, and wildlife of the entire estuary and the Quashnet River Valley.

Citizen groups formed in the early 1980s and have fought with the military base to clean up the damage they had done to the aquifer. After a 20-year effort, they have achieved a number of victories. Through their efforts the military is listed as the major polluter of 70% of the drinking water on Cape Cod. Cleanup is under way on several of the contamination plumes, but more work needs to be done. It was these group efforts that led to the cleanup purification system now in place at Mashpee-owned cranberry bogs on the upper Quashnet River. Other citizen groups continue to fight and debate the high rates of various cancers and their causes, but are met with increasing resistance from questionable government reports.

The Cape Cod Commission, a Regional Planning Board to oversee development and the environment on Cape Cod, was envisioned, first, by Cape Cod citizen groups, embraced by some state lawmakers, authorized by voters, and then commissioned by state law in 1990. Not a year goes by when the Cape Cod Commission fails to be under attack by business interests, town politicians, public officials, and developers. More citizen groups are forming as they realize they must take the power back from officialdom if they are to make headway with the Cape Cod environment. A new citizen group has formed demanding the restoration of the devastated Coonamesset River. If this river was restored it could rival the Mashpee and the Quashnet for quality sea run brook trout fishing.

Our Fish and Wildlife Division has taken more ownership of assisting with the restoration of the sea run brook trout fisheries. They have transferred wild sea run brook trout from the Quashnet River to the nearby Childs River in hopes of creating a population there. They are now encouraging removal of dams and better fish passageways. They assist on restoration work and are working to document river flows, fish migration, insect life, and river temperatures, which are all so important when battling the positions of those who resist the needed reforms. They are working on a project to return sea run brook trout to the historic Eel River in Plymouth, Massachusetts, where the recreated 1621 Plymouth Plantation is located.

Red Brook, a historic sea run brook trout river in Wareham across the Cape Cod Canal, has been donated by the Lyman family. With initial help from the Cape Cod Chapter of TU (now the Trout Unlimited Southeast Chapter) through their coordinator Warren Winders, progress on its restoration is being made. The private Lyman family farmhouse on the river holds tracings of 19th century sea run brook trout caught in this river ranging upwards of 18 inches! The abutting cranberry grower A.D. Makepeace just allowed the acquisition of 245 acres of adjacent river land, bringing the preserved total acreage for Red Brook to almost 900 acres. State Fisheries biologist Steve Hurley has become a driving supportive force behind this acquisition and sea run brook trout restoration projects on both Cape Cod and in Southeastern Massachusetts.

Trout Unlimited National is giving growing attention to Cape Cod and its potential as a sea run brook trout fishery. The National Oceanic and Atmospheric Administration (NOAA) has taken interest in studying sea run brook trout from its Woods Hole location on Cape Cod.

An anti-herbicide citizens group has formed to attempt to stop the needless damaging herbicide usage by the new British owners of NSTAR (our electric utility company) but they are being met with great resistance from the company and receive little local, state and federal agency support.

Efforts by other citizen groups from Cape Cod have received support from the state Attorney General, who has now taken over responsibility of the open meeting law enforcement on Cape Cod. The decision by the AG to prosecute officials for breaking the laws regarding open meetings will have a long term positive effect for the Cape Cod environment. Another Cape Cod citizens group, Citizens for Homeowners Insurance Reform has successfully fought the political system and won a major victory with the support of the Attorney General. Although this group was not focused on the environment, they proved what citizens groups can accomplish against a political and business establishment that has had its own way for hundreds of years.

We will need to build upon citizens groups and their work in order to gain more support from all the governments and their agencies in our efforts to restore the environment of Cape Cod for its people and its sea run brook trout.

We can follow the path set by Fran Smith on the Quashnet, Warren Winders on Red Brook, and Steve Hurley of the Fisheries Division as examples of actual stream habitat restoration, and apply these lessons to other Cape Cod rivers in need such as the Marstons Mills River, Little River, the Santuit, Quaker Run, Little Red Brook, the Childs River, Coonamesset River, Mill Creek, Scorton Creek in Sandwich, the Herring River in Harwich, and the Pamet River in Truro, along with a score of smaller brooks and streams across Cape Cod that all historically had fishable populations of sea run brook trout.

In doing so, we would create a world class sea run brook trout fishery here on Cape Cod and it may become a trout fishing destination. This would develop business and tax revenues because anglers and their families spend money on hotels, resorts, boating, clothing, shopping, and licensing. With a world class sea run brook trout fishery anglers may be more easily persuaded to relocate here and purchase homes.

Once again, if we have sea run brook trout, then we will have healthy estuaries with both commercial and recreational shellfishing. We will maintain healthy herring and eel populations resulting in good lobster, crab, striped bass, and cod populations for commercial and recreational fishing, creating more sustainable year-round employment.

A major disappointment however is that, after 20 years of the existence of the Waquoit Bay Estuarine Reserve and Cape Cod Commission, there has not been any further stream restoration or rehabilitation beyond what has been achieved by the Cape Cod Chapter of Trout Unlimited and Fran Smith and his volunteers on the Quashnet. We have not added a new river nor have we completed restoration of the Quashnet River. The Town of Mashpee has not undertaken the needed Mashpee River restoration and it seems we are in a holding pattern at a time we should be moving forward.

Howard Zinn, a writer and historian, who had spent a great deal of time on Cape Cod and was instrumental in founding the Wellfleet Harbor Actor's Theatre, passed away recently. Interviewed shortly before his death by a Cape Cod reporter, he expressed his disappointment in the actions and in the lack of action by our governments and their agencies. But he expressed renewed hope in the success that citizen action groups have begun to achieve here on Cape Cod. He believed, as did Eleanor Roosevelt, that real change must come from the person on the street upward and cannot be expected to come from government down.

It is my belief that, in order to recreate and restore the historic sea run brook trout rivers of Cape Cod, each river system must have its own citizens action group. We can not expect it to happen by merely sitting back and waiting for government agencies to take the necessary action. The last 25 years has demonstrated that nothing positive will happen unless the average citizen steps up to the plate. It is challenging. I have experienced defeat at open meetings. And I will tell you we are up against major obstacles.

My further belief is that we should establish our own sea run brook trout institute on Cape Cod with its focus on restoring sea run brook trout to all Cape waters. In conjunction with that, we should establish a stream rehabilitation company, which can accomplish the difficult habitat work. Both entities could be established as non-profits. The reason is that NOAA, EPA, Waquoit Bay Reserve and others, although of immense assistance, have rather large agendas of which our sea run brook trout are only a very small part. It is too easy for the plight of the trout to get lost or compromised by so many other seemingly more important aspects of projects. We need to take charge of these efforts ourselves. In the process we would develop jobs for the Cape's economy. With 20 or more rivers needing a wide variety of restoration, rehabilitation, and maintenance, the work will go on for decades to come. And what is learned here on Cape Cod could be exported to assist in such restoration projects anywhere.

Humanity has a long history of failed civilizations all around the globe. The belief is they all grew too big and overextended themselves and their environments, causing eventual collapse. Are we doing the same? Is it not the time to begin to truly preserve, restore, and rehabilitate the air, the water, the environment, and our sea run brook trout? It will be a major task. It cannot be done without major land and water use changes, and will require a concerted citizen effort. We only have two partial, fragile river systems left. We have proven they can be preserved but the even bigger vision is to utilize them to restore the twenty plus rivers lost. In undertaking such an effort we will be benefitting our children and future generations.

The late John Hay wrote *The Run* in 1959, a book about ocean herring migrating up Stony Brook near his home in Brewster on Cape Cod, to spawn in the river's lakes. The book tells the story of the gauntlet of obstacles from nature, predators, and man they must pass to spawn and then return to sea. They die by the thousands in this effort to recreate. Their little ones return to the sea where the survivors reach adulthood and return to Stony Brook's lakes to begin the cycle once again. It is a bittersweet story of the herring's life cycle, too often shortened by man's greed and interference. Mr. Hay went on to write in 1965 another Cape Cod classic *The Great Beach*, for which he was awarded the John Burroughs Medal, our nation's highest honor for nature writing.

I read *The Run* as a teenager before I had ever seen Cape Cod or knew what a herring was and before I ever heard of sea run brook trout. John Hay moved to Cape Cod at Brewster in 1946, the same year I was born. Disappointed in the rapid destruction of the Cape's resources, he left Cape Cod for the wilds of Maine in 1984, the same year I arrived as a wash ashore. He wrote 18 nature books and founded the Cape Cod Museum of Natural History.

Author Robert Finch, a famed nature writer from Wellfleet on Cape Cod, and a former neighbor of Hay summed up Hay's life in a 2011 obituary. "Part of his vision of the natural world was that it is not distinct from us as he could see in other species aspects of his own humanity." Finch said. "That's what led him to say that when we diminish the natural world, we diminish ourselves."

The rare Indian Pipe is found in the restored woodland valley of the upper Quashnet River. Another testimony to the value of river restoration efforts.

That insight and statement from Robert Finch affirms why we must work to restore what we have damaged.

Henry David Thoreau, while writing his classic *Walden* took vacation walking trips on Cape Cod during the 1850s. He spent his time exploring the beaches and marshes from Orleans to Wellfleet to Provincetown, often commenting on the treeless, barren, waste-like inland areas of Cape Cod, while enamored of wherever the sandy beaches met the sea. This stark contrast of man denuding the land of trees for firewood, building materials, and cranberry bogs against the vast ocean which man could not yet destroy, kept Thoreau coming back.

Thoreau lived to see *Walden* published, but his *Cape Cod* was published posthumously in 1864. Unfortunately, Thoreau never explored the Mashpee and Quashnet River valleys, robbing us of the insight he would have shared. In what were to become some of the last words he would ever write, at the very end of *Cape Cod*, as Thoreau stood at an eastern sandy beach looking out across the great Atlantic Ocean, he wrote, "A man may stand there and put all of America behind him."

The culture of greed and its pollution of America has marched its way back and forth across America and continues to re-emerge on Cape Cod. It is time we draw the line in the sand and say, "No more." Instead of tolerating the killing waters, we need to rise up and restore all our Cape Cod sea run brook trout rivers into healing waters.

Dana Lamb, a trout and salmon fly-fisher who wrote over a dozen books on the subject and donated a portion of his profits to river restoration, was asked in an interview if it was worth trying to restore damaged and devastated trout and salmon rivers.

"Can it be done?" he responded. "We don't know for certain. But a man's reach should exceed his grasp or what's a heaven for?"

Chapter Twenty

MAY THERE BE NO ENDING

I have the good fortune to live in a 40-year old cottage on a trout pond. The pond is stocked twice a year by the Massachusetts Fisheries Division and from my canoe I take pleasures in fly-fishing for its stocked and holdover rainbow and brown trout. From this "Trout Cottage," as I refer to it, I am just minutes away from the Mashpee and Quashnet Rivers.

On stormy evenings, I will alternate from a warm seat by its living room fireplace to the cold, wind and rain swept, screened porch outside. There in the wind and wetness, if I listen closely enough, I can hear the waves of Nantucket Sound crashing against the barrier dunes just a few miles away (as the crow flies) from Centerville to Osterville and Cotuit and beyond. Once I am wet and cold enough, I retreat back inside to the warmth of the fire and a libation.

On such evenings, the strong winds lash across the pond and rain pounds onto the windows and roof, cascading down like so many tiny waterfalls. The gutters and downspouts become overwhelmed and the racket of splashing waters rule out sleep. The towering spruces, pines, and hemlocks groan and strain and a few weaker branches and limbs give way, cracking then crashing to the ground or roof. The laurels, hollys, and rhododendrons swing and sway wildly about before springing back to their natural position, like a bamboo rod completing its cast.

I can't sleep, but I am not sure whether it is because I am going sea run brook trout fishing in the morning, which is always like Christmas morning excitement to me, or the storm's rage. I know I love them both. So who needs sleep when contemplating a day on the Mashpee or the Quashnet?

The full moon peeks through occasional dark rain cloud openings reminding me that there will be a super high tide in the estuaries. I welcome the downpours knowing that a sudden flush of rainwater down our rivers, combined and met with estuary high tides often brings a fresh run of silver blue brookies upriver from the brackish saltwater. This greatly improves the chances of catching one of the rare 12- to 14-inch sea runs.

I rummage through my tackle vest and fly boxes looking for the flies that will be the most effective. I sharpen their hook points and arrange them in an order that only makes sense to me. Then I string up the little 6-foot rod and clean the line. Once satisfied I relax in my chair contemplating the promise of the morning's fishing, the river I will visit, the beauty of a fly-fishing life, and the historic lives of past Cape Cod fly-fishers.

My reveries drift back to a time when the road beyond the cottage was dirt and gravel and the mode of transportation was horse and wagon. It was a time before all the houses, trophy homes, strip malls, shopping centers, and commercial, box-like buildings. The Centerville and Marstons Mills Rivers, just yards away from "Trout Cottage," would have harbored runs of sea run brook trout that have now been extinct for over a century.

I can picture Daniel Webster, who traveled from his estate in nearby Marshfield, and spent the night at the Inn in Sandwich which now bears his name, rising at dawn and being transported by horse and wagon for a day of fishing on the Mashpee or Quashnet. He would spend the day in solitude on the river fishing a "little 8-foot fly rod" as recommended for fishing the Mashpee and Quashnet by Dr. Jerome Smith in his 1833 book *Fishes of Massachusetts*. This was quite radical as, at the time, most fly rods were 10 to 12 feet long, as is Webster's rod that is on display at the American Museum of Fly Fishing in Manchester, Vermont! Daniel Webster would use a horse hair leader and braided line, swinging a two wet fly setup (likely a Soldier Palmer and a Coachman) through the river's pockets and runs. On a regular basis he would catch sea run brook trout in the 12- to 16-inch range. He would take a ploughman's lunch break with apples, sourdough bread, cheddar cheese, and ale, and would drink thirstily from one of the scores of springs entering the river. With a tin cup and a small fire he would brew a cup of tea and finish with a libation from his leather-covered flask.

An autumn 11" silver blue sea run brook trout that recently migrated into the freshwater of the lower Mashpee River from the saltwater estuary. It was quickly released back to the river.

Satiated with his fishing success, he would rest under a stand of pine and hemlock and take a notebook from his shoulder bag and write one of his now historic speeches in quietude. The only sounds would be the gentle background music of songbirds, gurgling water, and rising trout, softened by the rush of a breeze through the boughs overhead.

When the driver came to meet him at the appointed hour and location he would ride the bouncing wagon with the creaking axle back to the inn for a hot bath, a warm fire, dinner, libations, tea, one of his famous "Debates with the Devil," followed by a restful, peaceful sleep that only a fly-fisher of trout from these little rivers can know.

I lament that the quietude and solitude of Daniel Webster's day is gone forever from these Cape Cod rivers. Today when one fishes these rivers, the noise and rush of auto and truck traffic often seeps through the woods overlaying the sounds of songbirds and gurgling waters. The sudden rumbling, explosive noise of jet planes from the nearby military base shocks the angler as they seem to roar by at tree level shaking the ground and the very river itself. The not-distant-enough, muffled sounds of leaf blowers, lawnmowers, and chainsaws from the ever encroaching suburban housing developments beyond the riverbanks, may be out of sight, but within ear shot. Now, drinking from a spring along the river is wrought with danger from the unknown chemicals and septic micro organisms you may be ingesting.

And yet, despite man's chaotic, noisy, seemingly mindless, rushing comings and goings, his ignorance of how to coexist with the environment, his continual direct and indirect pollution of the rivers, and his destruction of the forests adjoining these little river valleys, the trout are still here.....for now.

They are not, mind you, in the numbers or the size of Daniel Webster's day. A fly-fisher learns to compartmentalize and ignore the ugly sounds of man's activities. But if one listens long enough and quietly enough the sounds of songbirds, the flush of grouse, the bob white call of quail, rising trout, and wind through trees will be heard.

These little rivers are a microcosm of damage done and ongoing damage to our trout rivers across our country. The only difference is that our Cape Cod waters are smaller in size but large in heart, hope and spirit.

In spite of some recent hopeful signs I still fear for the future of these little rivers and their unique sea run brook trout. My hope is that they will be here for future generations to enjoy these waters and their speckled inhabitants.

They have no voice. They can not speak for themselves. Only we can speak for them.

May there be no ending to their story.

SELECTED BIBLIOGRAPHY

My personal library collection of fly-fishing and related works has grown to over 1,000 books. Fly-fishing literature worldwide totals in the thousands. The following listing from my collection is focused on those authors and their works that mainly influenced *A Tale of Two Rivers* but are by no means an all inclusive list of the many American & British authors who have contributed to my half century of a fly-fishing life.

AMERICAN AUTHORS

Bates, Joseph D., Jr. *Streamer Fly Tying & Fishing*. Mechanicsburg, PA: Stackpole, 1950, 1986, 1995.

Bolling, David M. *How To Save A River.* Washington, D.C.: Island, 1994.

Carson, Rachel. *Silent Spring.* Boston: Houghton Mifflin, 1962.

Caucci, Al and Nastasi, Bob. *Hatches*. New York: Comparahatch, 1978.

Cleveland, Grover. *Fishing and Shooting Sketches*. New York: Curtis, 1901; New York: Arno, 1966.

Dalton, Stephen. *At The Water's Edge*. New York: Portland, 1989.

Elliot, Bob. *The Eastern Brook Trout*. New York: Norton, 1950.

Flick, Art. *Streamside Guide to Naturals and Their Imitations.* NY: Crown, 1970.

Gill, Emlyn M. *Practical Dry Fly-fishing*. New York: Scribners, 1913.

Gingrich, Arnold, editor. *American Trout Fishing.* New York: Knopf, 1966.

Gordon, Theodore. *The Complete Fly-Fisherman. The Notes and Letters of Theodore Gordon.* John McDonald, editor. New York: Scribners, 1947.

Garrison, Everett and Carmichael, Hoagy. *A Master's Guide to Building a Fly Rod.* New York: Martha's Glen, 1977.

Gates, David Alan. *Seasons of the Salt Marsh.* Connecticut: Chatham, 1975.

Hay, John. *The Run*. New York: Doubleday, 1959

Herrick, William. "A Battenkill Funeral." From *Anthology. American Trout Fishing.* Gingrich, Arnold, editor. New York: Knopf, 1966.

Hilyard, Graydon R. and Leslie K. *Carrie G. Stevens.* PA: Stackpole, 2000.

Humphrey, William. *The Spawning Run*. New York: Knopf, 1970

Jennings, Preston. *A Book of Trout Flies*. New York: Crown, 1970.

Karas, Nick. *Brook Trout.* New York: Lyons & Burford, 1997.

Keane, Martin J. *Classic Rods and Rodmakers.* New York: Winchester, 1976.

Koch, Ed. *Fishing the Midge.* New York: Freshet, 1972.

_____. *Terrestrial Fishing*. PA: Stackpole, 1990.

La Branche, George M. L. *The Dry Fly and Fast Water.* New York: Scribner, 1914.
Lamb, Dana S. *Some Silent Places Still.* Massachusetts: Barre, 1969.
_____. *Where The Pools Are Bright and Deep*. New York: Winchester, 1973.
_____. *Beneath The Rising Mist*. Boston: Stone Wall, 1979
Leisenring, James E. *The Art of Tying the Wet Fly*. New York: Dodd Mead, 1944.
Leisenring, James E., and Hidy, Vernon S. *The Art of Tying the Wet Fly and Fishing the Flymph.* New York: Crown, 1971.
Marbury, Mary Orvis. *Favorite Flies and Their Histories*. New Jersey: Wellfleet, 1988. Reprint of 1892 edition.
Mares, William. *Fishing With the Presidents.* Mechanicsburg, PA: Stackpole, 1999.
Marinaro, Vincent. *A Modern Dry Fly Code*. New York: Crown, 1970.
_____. *In The Ring Of The Rise.* New York: Crown, 1976.
McCade, Britton C., DR., and Swartz, Albert H. *Fisheries Report on Barnstable County Of 1948*. Boston: Commonwealth of MA, 1951.
McDonald, John. *The Origins of Angling*. New York: Lyons & Burford, Reprint (1963).
Merwin, John. *The Battenkill.* New York: Lyons and Burford, 1993.
Morris, Holly, Editor. *Uncommon Waters-Women Write About Fishing*. Seattle: Seal, 1991.
Nemes, Sylvester. *The Soft-Hackled Fly.* Connecticut: Chatham, 1975.
Norris, Thaddeus. *The American Angler's Book*. NY: Derrydale, 1864. (Reprint)
Ovington, Ray. *Tactics On Trout.* New York: Knopf, 1969.
_____. *How To Take Trout On Wet Flies and Nymphs*. New York: Freshet, 1974.
Rhead, Louis. *The Speckled Brook Trout*. New York: Derrydale, 1902. (Reprint)
Sargent, William. *Shallow Waters.* Boston: Houghton Mifflin, 1981.
Schullery, Paul. *American Fly-fishing—A History.* New York: Lyons, 1987.
Schwiebert, Earnest. *Matching the Hatch*. New York: Macmillan, 1955.
_____. *Remembrances of Rivers Past*. New York: Macmillan, 1972.
_____. *Nymphs.* New York: Winchester, 1973.
_____. *Trout.* Volume I and II. New York: Dutton, 1978.
_____. *Death of a Riverkeeper.* New York: Dutton, 1980.
_____. *A River For Christmas.* Lexington, MA: Greene, 1988.
_____. *The Compleat Schwiebert.* John Merwin, editor. New York: Dutton 1990.
_____. *Nymphs*—Volume I: The Mayflies. CT: Lyons, 2007.
_____. *Nymphs*—Volume II: Stoneflies, Caddisflies and Other Insects. Lyons, 2007.
Shaw, Helen. *Flies For Fish and Fishermen*. PA: Stackpole, 1989.
Smith, Jerome V. C. M.D. *A Natural History of the Fishes of Massachusetts.* Boston: Allen and Ticknor, 1833 (Reprint).
Thoreau, Henry David. *Cape Cod*. Orleans, MA: Parnassus, 1984. Reprint of the 1864 edition.
Traver, Robert. *Anatomy of a Fisherman*. New York: McGraw-Hill, 1964.
_____. *Trout Madness.* New York: Peregrine Smith, 1970 Reprint of the 1960 edition by St. Martin press.
_____. *Trout Magic*. New York: Crown, 1974.
Van Dyke, Henry. *Little Rivers.* New York: Scribner, 1908.
Webster, Daniel. *The Writings and Speeches of Daniel Webster In Eighteen Volumes.* Boston: Little Brown & Company, 1903. Limited Edition. From the Private Library Collection of Robert A. Bianchi

Wilson, Francis. *Joseph Jefferson.* New York: Scribner, 1906.
Wright, Leonard M. Jr. *Fishing the Dry Fly as a Living Insect.* New York: Dutton, 1972.

BRITISH ISLES AUTHORS

Berners, Dame Juliana. *A Treatise on Fishing with a Hook*. New York: North River, Translation Reprint 1979 of the 1496 Westminster Edition.
Bingham, Charles. *Chalk Stream Salmon & Trout Fishing*. Shrewsbury, England: Swan Hill, 1993.
Clapham, Richard. *Trout Fishing on Hill Streams*. Edinburgh & London: Oliver & Boyd,1947.
Falkus, Hugh. *Sea Trout Fishing.* London: Witherby, 1986 Second Edition reprint of 1962 revised edition of 1981.
Greene, Harry Plunket. *Where The Bright Waters Meet.* London: Witherby, 1969. Reprint of the 1924 Allan edition.
Haig-Brown, Roderick L. *Return To The River.* New York: Morrow, 1941.
_____. *A River Never Sleeps*. New York: Morrow, 1944.
_____. *Fisherman's Spring.* New York: Morrow, 1951.
_____. *Fisherman's Fall.* New York: Morrow, 1954.
_____. *Fisherman's Winter.* New York: Morrow, 1954.
_____. *Fisherman's Summer.* New York: Morrow, 1959.
_____. *To Know A River.* New York: Lyons & Burford, 1996.
Halford, Frederic M. *Dry Fly-fishing.* Reading, England: Shurlock,1973 Reprint of the 1889 edition.
Hall, John Inglis. *Fishing a Highland Stream.* Middlesex, England and New York, USA: Viking Penguin, 1987. Reprint of the 1960 Edition.
Hills, John Waller. *A Summer on the Test.* Reading, England: Shurlock, 1972 Fifth printing of the 1924 edition.
_____. *A History of Fly-fishing For Trout.* London: Allan, 1921. Reprint 1974 by Freshet Press, New York.
King, Patricia. *Muriel Foster's Fishing Diary*. London & New York: Viking, 1980.
Kite, Major Oliver. *Nymph Fishing In Practice.* London: Jenkins, 1963.
Paterson, Wilma and Behan, Prof. Peter. *Salmon & Women.* London: Witherby, 1990.
Patterson, Neil. *Chalkstream Chronicle.* UK: Merlin Unwin, 1995 and USA: Lyons & Burford, 1995.
Robson, Kenneth Editor. *The Essential G. E. M. Skues.* London: Black, 1998.
Ronalds, Alfred. *The Fly-Fisher's Entomology.* USA: Wellfleet, 1990. Reprint of the 1836 London edition.
Sawyer, Frank. *Keeper of the Stream.* London: Adam & Charles, 1952.
_____. *Nymphs and the Trout.* London: Stanley Paul, 1958.
Skues, G. E. M. *Minor Tactics of the Chalk Stream.* London: Black, 1910.
_____. *The Way of a Trout With a Fly.* London: Black, 1921.
_____. *Sidelines, Sidelights and Reflections.* London: Seeley Service, 1932.
Taverner, Eric. *The Making of a Trout Stream.* London: Seeley Service, 1953.
Walker, C. F. Brown *Trout and Dry Fly.* London: Seeley Service, 1955.
Wilson, Dermot. *Fishing the Dry Fly.* London: Black, 1970.

ORGANIZATIONS, MUSEUMS, & FLY-FISHING TACKLE SUPPLIERS

American Museum of Fly Fishing
4104 Main Street
Manchester VT 05254
www.amff.com

Cape Cod Commission
3225 Main Street
Barnstable, MA 02630
www.capecodcommission.org

Cape Cod Conservation Trusts
3239 Main Street
Barnstable, MA 02630
www.compact.cape.com

Cape Cod Trout Unlimited
www.capecodtu.org

Casting for Recovery
3738 Main Street
Manchester, VT 05254
www.castingforrecovery.org

Catskill Fly-fishing Museum
1031 Old Route 17
Livingston Manor, NY 12758
www.cffcm.net

Fishing The Cape
www.fishingthecape.com

Hardy North America
1260 Corporate Blvd
Lancaster, PA 17601
www.hardynorthamerica.com

International Federation of Fly-fishers
5237 U.S. Highway 89 South, Suite 11
Livingston, MT 59047
www.fedflyfishers.org

International Women Fly-fishers
www.intlwomenflyfishers.org

L.L. Bean
15 Casco Street
Freeport, ME 04032
www.llbean.com

Orvis Company
4180 Main Street
Manchester VT 05254
www.orvis.com/manchester

Rangeley Outdoor Sporting Heritage Museum
Main Street
Oquossoc, Maine
www.rangeleyoutdoormuseum.org

Regal Engineering
100 Prentiss Street
Orange, MA 01364
www.regalvise.com

Silent Spring Institute
29 Crafts Street
Newton, MA 02458
info@silentspring.org

Trout Unlimited National Office
1300 N. 17TH St.
Arlington, VA 22209-2404
www.tu.org

Waquoit Bay National Estuarine Reserve
149 Waquoit Highway
Waquoit, MA 02536
www.waquoitbayreserve.org

INDEX